The Limitations of Social Research

M.D. Shipman B.Sc. (Soc.), Ph.D.

Senior Lecturer in Education
University of Keele

Longman

LONGMAN GROUP LIMITED
London
*Associated companies, branches and representatives
throughout the world*

First published 1972
Second impression 1975

ISBN 0582 48049 3 Paper
48050 7 Cased

*Printed in Hong Kong by
The Continental Printing Co Ltd*

Aspects of modern sociology

Social research

GENERAL EDITORS

John Barron Mays
Eleanor Rathbone Professor of Sociology, University of Liverpool

Maurice Craft
Senior Lecturer in Education, University of Exeter

The Sociology of the School (1968)
Education and Modernisation (1971)

Contents

Editors' Preface

The first series in Longman's *Aspects of Modern Sociology* library was concerned with the social structure of modern Britain, and was intended for students following professional and other courses in universities, polytechnics, colleges of education, and elsewhere in further and higher education, as well as for those members of a wider public wishing to pursue an interest in the nature and structure of British society.

This further series sets out to examine the history, aims, techniques and limitations of social research, and it is hoped that it will be of interest to the same readership. It will seek to offer an informative but not uncritical introduction to some of the methodologies of social science.

JOHN BARRON MAYS
MAURICE CRAFT

Acknowledgements

We are grateful to the following for permission to reproduce copyright material:
To Harvard University Press for an extract from *The Failures of Economics* by S. Schoeffler.

Foreword

Most of the books on the methods of social investigation have been written for the small minority who will go on to do their own research. The purpose of this book is to provide a guide for the majority, not on how to design social investigations, but on how to assess the reliability of research that has been reported in books and articles. It is addressed to three main groups. First, to those who use the evidence from the social sciences, particularly sociology. Second, to students of social science who are often taught as potential producers of new evidence but rarely helped to become informed critics of existing work. Third, to the general public, to whom it offers a view of the way evidence is produced in, and presented by, scientific communities.

The conventional approach tends to reinforce the false impression that research consists of standardised techniques applied at predetermined stages. Such neatness is rare in practice. Humans are not passive objects but interact with the researcher and often frustrate him. Yet the formal presentation of results often covers up accident prone research. In more advanced works, elementary warnings about the limitations of research recorded in articles and theses are omitted, and the theories from which research techniques have originated are taken for granted. Lastly, there is rarely any discussion of the way social scientific communities stage manage their public image.

This book is organised in the same sequence as the research it reports. Chapters 1, 2, and 3 probe the influences on the social scientist as he works. Chapters 4 to 8 cover the technical stages of research. Chapters 9 to 12 describe the conventions governing the relations between scientists and their public in order to explain the way results are presented. At this stage polemic and generalisation abound, just as they do in the concluding passages of many research reports. The limitations of social research are illustrated by eight Controversies, each involving evidence collected by methods discussed in the text. The Controversies have been chosen for their central importance within Education.

Three key questions recur in all chapters. They should be asked about this book as well as others.

KEY QUESTION 1

If the investigation had been carried out by someone other than the author, using his methods, would the same results have been obtained?
The concern here is with the reliability of the methods used. This includes a consideration of the instruments used for gathering information and the dependability of the researcher. Instruments such as questionnaires and interviews used in the social sciences are never completely reliable and there are always opportunities for distortion through the influence of the investigator and his interaction with the subjects of the study.

KEY QUESTION 2

Do the results really reflect the influence of the factors under examination or did extraneous influences interfere?
The concern here is with internal validity. The ideal experiment has all variables under control so that the effect of varying one can be investigated. This is sometimes possible in the natural sciences, but unlikely where humans are the subjects. Humans are expert in detecting clues about possible responses and it is difficult to control or randomise the consequences. This is complicated by the interaction of the researcher and the subjects as each gives, receives and acts on clues. Finally there is a limit to the extent to which humans can be restrained in the interests of controlled research.

KEY QUESTION 3

What relevance do the results have beyond the actual research?
The concern here is with external validity, the extent to which results can be generalised. The research situation, because it has to be controlled, is necessarily artificial. Samples may be too small or unrepresentative. Individuals under observation tend not to behave naturally. Results from research in any one place or at any one time may not be applicable in others. Children of one age, schools of one size, members of one group may be a misleading source if observations of them are taken as typical of others. Human individuals and human groups are marked by their variety. Generalisation from one to another may be misleading.

The ability to answer these questions is necessary to all who use, study or just enjoy social science. Examples have been chosen from Education because the issues there are typical of subjects where evidence from social science is used, but where the discipline that shaped the research producing the evidence was not shared by the users. Students are not alone in having to accept evidence without knowledge of the way it was actually produced. The motto is therefore *caveat emptor*, let the buyer beware. The book should be read in this spirit, for it too is the work of a social scientist presenting a selection of evidence to prove his case.

Thanks are due to Eugene Ring and Marion Jordan who exposed many of the grosser prejudices of the author in earlier drafts and to Professor R.J. Frankenberg who showed how many still remained at the end.

M.D. SHIPMAN

Scientific activity in theory and practice

The view taken in this book is that science is organised as both a mystery and a discipline. Both are aspects of the existence of scientific communities that manage their internal affairs and external relations. The mystery enables scientists to exclude the public from influence over their work. The discipline is exercised by scientists over one another as problems for study, procedures for research and the form for reporting results are chosen. Most of this book is concerned with the consequences of the adoption of this model by social scientists. The combination of insulation from lay influence and simultaneous exposure to the judgment of colleagues is seen as the source both of the strength of science and of public misunderstandings about it.

Science has not resulted in the steady accumulation of proven facts giving an increasingly complete and true picture of the natural world. The history of science has consisted of apparently watertight theories being punctured and replaced by others which satisfactorily incorporate the cause of the puncture. Of the two major writers in this field, Popper sees this recurrence of revolutions as the result of the ruthless scepticism of scientists towards existing evidence.[1] Kuhn by contrast sees this scepticism being directed, not against established theories and procedures but against other scientists as they work to add missing pieces to accepted theoretical models.[2] However, whether scepticism is directed at established knowledge or against professional competence, it is anticipated and exercised by scientists. The price of entry into a scientific community is this acceptance that the final judgment of new work will come through agreement among established fellow professionals.

The acceptance of evidence only after scrutiny and agreement by scientific elites has implications for scientific procedures. There has never been a single, standardised scientific method. The constant element has been the exposure of new evidence and new scientists to the judgment of established members of the relevant community. This recognition motivates the ambitious and is the reward for accepting the exposure. Qualification for full membership comes through examination, not only in basic theoretical knowledge, but in displaying competence in research at the higher degree level. Recognition comes through satisfying editors and referees of reputable journals that work is worth publishing.

Communities of scientists as elsewhere are organised into hierarchies of authority and prestige.[3] Most books deal only with the small group at the centre of communication and influence. This group enjoy full knowledge of the mystery and control over the discipline. Around this central group, usually based in the universities, are larger groups concerned more with the use than with the advancement of scientific knowledge. They are outside the informal network of communication that links those at the centre and have a restricted view of the way new evidence is produced. Finally, around the frontiers of each scientific community are the public, including students qualifying for entry. Here the communal private language, the conventions governing the reporting of research, are not fully understood and the image obtained is that presented from within.

This communal structure is the key to the accumulation of knowledge through science. It ensures the exclusion of the bogus. But it can also mystify the public. It can lend communal support to individual scientists. But it can also lead to conformity through the need for the newcomer to satisfy established colleagues, through their control over funds, facilities, journals and examinations. Textbooks may confirm the impression that there exist unchallenged theories with unbroken histories. Normal science may not only be disciplined, but consist of the routine investigation of problems that are known to be soluble in the light of existing knowledge.

This is not the image presented to the public or to students. The window-dressing can be seen in the layout of the scientific paper. Medawar has argued that such papers are frauds because they suggest that the observations made in the experiment impinged on an open mind.[4] Only then is there a discussion of the meaning of the results obtained. In reality all scientific enquiry starts with expectations about the outcome. The scientist selects his problem, designs his research and analyses his results by reference to existing theory. The key stage in research, the formulation of hypotheses, consists of hunches derived in this way. Science is normally problem solving, not a thrust into the unknown.

Medawar is drawing a distinction between two parts of scientific research. There is the inspiration, creation, imagination and guesswork that finally leads to a hypothesis. There is then deduction from this hunch, followed by a second stage that can be a rigorous process of testing of the ideas. Both come from within the same discipline. But the real sequence of scientific research is inspiration then observation, not observation then inspiration as implied in streamlined written papers. Normal science consists of problem solving with the results anticipated because they will fit into the existing jigsaw. The imaginative stage occurs as the problem is first defined. As the data is collected it impinges on a mind already anticipating it. The scientific paper reverses the real sequence in order to preserve the impression of science as an inductive activity.

This convention for reporting science is part of the mystery that obscures the actual organisation of science from the public. It is not only that scientific communities develop private conventions for reporting research, private languages, professional associations and professional journals, but that within each community there are few at the centre of communications, prestige and power and many on the periphery. The producers of evidence tend to be central where the funds for research are available. On the fringes of the community are the wholesalers,

3

including the teachers, using this evidence, often in subjects centred outside and with a restricted view of actual production. Finally there are the consumers, whether students hoping to gain entry or the lay public, who have to take reliability and validity on trust. In doing so they are taught to accept the conventions. Only the few students who take higher degrees, find a sponsor for research, and are accepted into the academic life at the centre get to see the reality behind the presented picture.

SCIENTIFIC INQUIRY IN THEORY

There follow the conventional stages in scientific inquiry. In practice these are mingled with flashes of insight which may often change the direction of the work or lead to jumping backward or forward one or more steps. Moreover, it is rare to progress smoothly through the stages without meeting obstacles. Ingenuity and tenacity are often needed for completion.

1. *The creative stage.*

(*a*) Meeting a problem.
(*b*) The formulation of a hypothesis.
(*c*) Deduction from the hypothesis.

This stage is creative because a scientist is not only alert to the existence of examinable problems, but can relate the possibility of a solution to the theory of his discipline. His initial hunch is the link between theory and problem. His deductions from that hunch employ concepts that are the core of his discipline. Finally he can formulate a hypothesis that he can test and others can assess and replicate.

2. *The technical stage*

(*a*) Designing the investigation.
(*b*) Collecting the data.

The technical stage is primarily concerned with ensuring reliability. It is at this stage that controls are established over possible extraneous variables, and errors in the means of collecting data are detected and eliminated. This usually means the use of a trial pilot run to test the techniques.

3. *The theoretical stage*

(*a*) Analysing the data.
(*b*) Drawing conclusions.

Analysis and generalisation bring the researcher back to the theories that originally produced the hypothesis. This is the reason why readers of research reports or those using the recommendations of scientists for making decisions should be able to relate the methods used back to the conceptual framework from which they originally sprang.

There are two important points about this model of research procedure. First, there is one technical stage sandwiched between two stages involving imagination. Scientific inquiry is not mechanical but creative. Secondly, the imagination used is bound within the subject discipline of the scientist concerned. The sociological imagination is not the same as the psychological. The quality of the research is largely determined by the nature of the discipline concerned and the quality of the theory that generated the imagination.

SCIENTISTS AT WORK

It is misleading to suggest that scientists work in the order set out earlier or finish with facts that are irrefutable. The actual process of research may follow no logical pattern. This reality is often concealed from the public. Scientists make their work public in a way that omits false starts, dead ends and changes in direction. Natural scientists and, increasingly, social scientists are members of communities and avoid exposing their criticisms of each other, however vicious these are in private. Communities within the social sciences may be less cohesive but the impression is still given to outsiders that members research according to established rules.

In this book the concern is with recognised, respectable and

5

publicised research. Below this, students and enthusiastic amateurs are active in practising the necessary techniques. Some consequences of this can be gauged in a study of ninety-eight anthropology students in California who were set an exercise in collecting information on a topic of their choice[5]. The consequences were described in an article titled "Unleashing the untrained". The author and organiser described the effect as "methodological and ethical violence". The choices ranged from examining the body beautiful to participant observation of drinking bouts. The students investigated relentlessly with a blatant disregard for the rights of others. They gave away confidences, acted as Peeping Toms, reported illegal practices, violated promised anonymity and obtained information by fraud. They obtained and used tests that required long training for proper administration. One stirred up an industrial dispute. The author cheerfully concluded that his students had done irreparable damage to the chances of those who might follow in the search for information. There is truly a Gresham's Law of research. The bad drives out the good.

This example could hardly be repeated in the natural sciences, where laboratories are supervised and dangerous objects kept locked up. The essence of reliable research is the extent of control exercised, not only over extraneous variables that could interfere in the relation being examined, but over the researcher himself. The controlled experiment in the natural sciences comes nearest perfect control. But even here the presence of the experimenter is a factor often influencing the experimental situation and his observations are subject to human error. But in the social sciences the observer not only has his weaknesses in perception, but is also liable to get involved with his subjects. Insight not control is often the feature of social scientific research. But insight means interaction, involvement and this is difficult to reconcile with the detached, objective stance traditionally adopted by scientists in their relations with the public.

The assessment of evidence in the social sciences depends on visualising the reality behind the written account of research. The reader should be an iconoclast, smashing the image of research as a methodical, consistent process following agreed rules of procedure. Visualise as a stimulus to such a sceptical attitude the work of McCaghy and Skipper published under the titles "Lesbian behaviour as an adaptation to the occupation of stripping" and "Stripteasers: the anatomy and career contingencies of a deviant occupation".[6] These two professors of sociology report that their observations and interviews took place in clubs and burlesque theatres in ten large cities located between Honolulu and New York, New Orleans and Chicago. Having watched the performance they were introduced to the girls backstage as professors doing an anthology on burlesque. Diligently making sure that they were both present they interviewed thirty-five strippers on the spot, or in a nearby bar or restaurant. The written account must have been dull compared with the actual fieldwork. Behind the table comparing the height, waist, bust and hip measurements of the sample, compared with Playboy Playmates of the month and the average American women may lie research activity rarely associated with scientists.

There are few studies of scientists at work.[7] Those there are give a very human picture of frustrations and joy, inspiration and depression, false starts and premature finishes. An example is Coleman's account of the progress of his work on "The adolescent society".[8] The start was a conversation between Coleman and Trow and their wives. Each had experienced a different type of schooling. This interested Coleman in the way prestige was allocated in high schools by the officials and by the adolescents. The first research proposals were written in 1954. Involvement in other work and a failure to obtain funds delayed the start until 1957.

Coleman's interest in the allocation of prestige was allied to his involvement in developing new methods of collecting data on social systems rather than individuals. However, when the analysis of data was started in 1958, it could not be used for its intended purpose. Coleman then changed the focus of the study from social system to role. Both the hypotheses and the methods of analysis were altered. The work was written in 1959, the manuscript was ready in 1960 and was published in 1961. In the seven years the work had changed, not only as a result of financial difficulties, but because the data did not live up to its promise.

Similar experiences were reported by Thomas and Znaniecki at a conference in 1938 arranged to discuss their book, *The Polish Peasant in Europe and America*, published twenty years before.[9] Thomas wanted to study immigrant problems, an important issue in North America in the early part of this century, and in 1908 received financial backing. He had the money and the hunch but no materials. His search for documentary evidence on Polish life involved adventures connected with the outbreak of the first world war that were not only unanticipated, but resulted in much material being left in a central European hotel by a courier fleeing from the authorities to avoid being called up for the army. Again, none of this farce appeared in the final books where the actual method of collecting the data was largely ignored. Indeed, Thomas admitted twenty years afterwards that the notes on methods in Volume 1 of the book were not based on the actual methods used, but were theoretical ideas developed by him as a lecturer. The conference organised by the Social Science Research Council in which the authors discussed their book and a critical commentary on it with other social scientists is unique. It is unlikely that many books would stand up as well to such examination, yet the impression remains of a published version that glossed over many shortcomings and included much that gave a false impression of meticulous scientific method. Similarly the generalisations made stretched far beyond those actually derived from the data. Finally, the retrospective comments by the two authors confirmed the common feeling of dissatisfaction with a work once it is in print.

These confusions and frustrations rarely appear in print. Books and articles consist of selections of successful investigations, pruned of those parts of the total work that did not lead to confirmation of a hypothesis. This convention probably does little harm within a profession that can interpret the written version, but by the time the article has been popularised in book form, any suggestions of irregularity are eliminated and the lay reader is given an impression of order that is very removed from actual practice.

The third exercise is to relate the popular versions of the research back to the original. Education is particularly open to the results of popularisation because it has to draw its information from a number of academic disciplines. The educationalist is outside the discipline in which the original work with which he is concerned was done. Consequently it is difficult to appreciate the specific difficulties that may have been met in the original research. An official report such as *Children and their Primary Schools*[10] has to blend actual practice in schools with developments in social science. Thus a chapter on children learning in school presents evidence from researchers such as Pavlov and Skinner, Isaacs and Piaget, and uses this to make statements about the value of play, discovery and activity. The work of social scientists are selected and then used to recommend some practices and discourage others, but without any discussion of the many criticisms of the selected work, or of the existence of alternative theories that could suggest different practices. Indeed, the social sciences are frequently used to justify existing fashion rather than as an objective basis for reform.

The incidental happenings in research are also pruned in writing up and only those steps which lead directly to proof or disproof of the hypothesis appear in the written report. The reasons for this retrospective falsification of changes of hypothesis, alterations in research design and the interference by uncontrolled peripheral influences lie primarily in the professional codes established in each academic discipline. In the social sciences particularly, the need to establish a position among the sciences necessitates a formality in reporting research that is often out of touch with the actual reliability of the procedures.

In practice chance occurrences during research have often proved more important than the original subject. Pasteur recognised that attenuated pathogens could be used for immunisation against disease as a result of trying to revive cultures which he had left while on vacation.[11] The most famous recent case has been Fleming's observations on the inhibition of bacterial growth by a mould which led to the development of penicillin. In all these cases it is the knowledge of the scientist which alerts him to the importance of the chance development. The term 'serendipity' was coined in the eighteenth century to describe this facility of researchers to exploit the chance discovery such as the *penicillium notatum* mould.

The existence of researchers willing to wander away from their mainstream of interest to pursue chance developments indicates a basic division among scientists. Some maintain that science should be imaginative and creative, while others support a science that follows clearly defined rules of procedure without deviation. The crucial perspective for the non-specialist is of science as an area of controversy and of scientists as fallible, argumentative, ambitious human beings like the rest of us, but constrained within often tight-knit communities. The examples from sociological research and from disputes over psychological and historical research cited later show the depth of this disagreement which is often concealed to the reader of books.

The way scientists actually work, and the impact of everyday matters upon their work can be gauged from the following case of the floppy-eared rabbits.[12] Two comparable medical scientists both noticed that rabbits injected with papain suffered from an amusing collapsing of the ears. Neither could devote much time to the phenomenon which did not seem to have any practical significance. However, one did try to obtain a rapid explanation of the ear collapse. He used his knowledge to do the expected tests. In reality these tests were selective, based on his ideas of what was likely to be the cause, the usual, but not the textbook procedure. He ignored the effect on cartilage because he had learned that this was not considered interesting. The other doctor too was amused, but used the ear collapse as a test of the potency of papain rather than trying to find a cause of the collapsing ears. Other work concerned with muscles also led him away from considering cartilage as the crucial area and also took up all his energy. The first doctor later chanced to show his students the collapse of the rabbit's ears and because he was in front of students he carried out the correct procedures rather than short-cutting according to his accumulated knowledge as he had done before and which was his, and other scientists', usual practice. Because he had more time at this moment, because he was getting students used to experimental pathology, and because there happened to be a large supply of rabbits available, he could carry out a systematic, controlled examination. By comparing injected and normal rabbits and taking sections from the ears of both he detected the change in the cartilage that provided the explanation.

These examples of serendipity lost and serendipity gained illustrate the way scientists use their knowledge of experimental variables to short-circuit textbook research procedures. In this case the knowledge of both doctors stopped them from looking at the cartilage which they considered unimportant and in which, because of the emphasis of their major research interests, they were not interested. Only when a teaching situation forced one to carry out formal comparisons between injected and normal rabbits was the rather obvious difference in cartilage revealed, much to the shame of the doctors concerned. Usually the short-circuiting is harmless. Scientific inquiry is rarely inductive, but always influenced by the preconceptions of the researcher which enable him to select among his data and concentrate on the important parts.

Social science

Natural and social scientists share a belief in the systematic and continual relation between theorising and the collection of evidence. Each scientific discipline constrains its members so that they select a distinctive range of phenomena to investigate and interpret their observations in distinctive ways. Each discipline has its own conceptual framework within which the scientist interprets his world as physicist, chemist, psychologist or sociologist. Similar phenomena may be observed by different scientists but the meanings given them will vary with the conceptual framework within which the interpretation takes place.

The major difference between natural and social science lies in the objects of study.[1] The natural scientist can impose his own definitions, order and control over his material. But the social scientist is involved with humans who have already interpreted their own world and are capable of responding actively to any attempt to impose scientific controls on their behaviour. Humans make themselves comfortable, secure and knowledgeable through common sense definitions of their world. They are fully capable of adjusting their behaviour and the meaning they give to events if a social scientist starts to investigate their lives. Being human is essentially having the capacity to manipulate the clues presented by others and to present clues to them in return. Instead of inert material for investigation the social scientist faces skilled manipulators of social situations.

There is a cartoon of a well-fed rat in a "Skinner Box" with a paw on a lever explaining to a fellow rat that he has the experimenter so well conditioned that every time he presses the lever the guy will push in food. Social scientific investigation always involves such interaction. Humans are skilled at creating impressions. The social scientist and the investigated both contribute their own meanings.

There are then two simultaneous processes of interpretation in social science. Ideally they should coincide. The social scientist trying to understand human behaviour has first to comprehend the existing, commonsense thinking of ordinary humans as they order their world. He builds his scientific theories on his understanding of the everyday, non-scientific lay order. To Schutz[2], concepts in social science are therefore constructs of constructs. But scientific models of related concepts are logical and general. Commonsense models are often illogical and always particular. A social scientist approaching households of husband, wife and mother-in-law has to try to get to know how each interprets their situation in the family. He relates his information to his discipline for his interpretation. But his theoretical model may be very different from the slippery, uncertain facts seen by those actually involved as they have to live with each other. Yet, initially the model was constructed through the social scientist's interpretation of everyday activity.

There is therefore a problem arising out of this coexistence of everyday and scientific frameworks for interpreting social activity. As a social scientist approaches a group or individual he becomes part of the situation he is investigating. Part of the behaviour he sees will be a response to his presence. As he tries to understand what goes on in the minds of his subjects, they are interpreting his presence, responding to him, offering him clues to test his response. The natural scientist need not worry about his gases. He manipulates them, controlling some factors in order to examine the relation between others. But the social scientist not only faces humans who are skilled at wriggling out of controls to establish their own areas of personal freedom, but is himself liable to create new adjustments that destroy the natural situation he is trying to understand.

There is therefore a clash between two essential parts of social scientific research, for involvement and detachment are contra-dictory. Involvement is necessary to make sense of the activity under investigation. Detachment is necessary for a scientist, not only to ensure reliable observation but to order the observations into the theoretical models that are the distinguishing feature of the discipline concerned. Only by this detached categorisation of particular items can general principles be established. But the social scientist cannot avoid involvement and consequently influences the very situation he is trying to investigate in a detached manner. This is a dilemma not faced by the natural scientist.

The task of the social scientist is therefore frequently to treat subjective meanings in an objective way. To Rickman, understand-ing, the process of getting to know the thoughts, feelings and motives of other humans, is involved in every operation in social scientific inquiry.[3] It enters into the formulation of hypotheses, the collection of data and into its interpretation. The natural scientist can abstract, relate, experiment and analyse without having to consider the reasons why gases act as they do. The social scientist is continually involved in this interpretative exercise. He is part of the experimental situation he creates, actively interpreting and acting as an important and often uncontrolled influence on the subjects of his research. He tries to understand the behaviour of others through knowledge of himself.

There are wide variations between the various social sciences and within each in the balance struck between involvement for understanding and detachment for reliability. Some (for example, anthropology) preserve the reality of the situation at all costs. Others (for example, experimental psychology) aim to reproduce the conditions of the controlled experiment, aiming to measure not interpret. However, whether the emphasis is on retaining spon-taneity or on maximising control, the collection of evidence and its interpretation occur simultaneously. The selection of a problem, the methods used to collect information on it, the tabulation and analysis of results all involve some interpretation, some under-standing of human behaviour in the area under investigation. The historian looking at documents, the psychologist measuring the sweat on the palm of his subject and the sociologist classifying cities along a rural–urban scale are all interpreting on the basis of their knowledge of the way men organise their behaviour. The product of their labours may be a detached description, generalisation or law but this is a product of their knowledge of the everyday world and the perspective that they use as followers of a particular discipline.

Nevertheless the rational model erected by the social scientist is part of normal scientific procedure. The scientist synthesises order out of the often disorderly activity that he observes. The distinguishing feature of social science is the degree to which tabulating, classifying, coding and analysing the data from observing human behaviour inevitably distorts it. Two schools of sociology, symbolic interactionism and ethnomethodology, have been concerned with probing the existence and consequences of this coincidence of inevitable interaction in social scientific research with the existence of a barrier between scientific and everyday concepts of the world.[4]

The human facility for using subtle responses in social interaction can be gauged from the work of Goffman.[5] Here the focus has been on the way men manage the impression they give to others in order to protect themselves and increase their advantage in the interaction. Silent, subtle adjustments are continually being made by those involved. This facility acts to erect barriers against social scientists trying to obtain insights into human behaviour. The observed are responding to the investigation and consequently distorting the image that they give to the observer.

More directly important for any discussion of social scientific methods has been the work of Garfinkel and Cicourel. Garfinkel has used his students to produce situations in which the normal rules of the game in everyday life are disturbed.[6] The students did not act according to the usual rules and the response was a breakdown in human intercourse. To Garfinkel these students were adopting the role of experimenters, disturbing the trust that rules relations between humans as they interact. Normal interaction became impossible. Garfinkel's conclusion from these experiments was that sociologists have ignored their own influence as participants in the situations they are investigating and have consequently erected rational models of behaviour that violate the actual pattern of often irrational, often disorganised, often absurd rules of the game of enabling life to continue.

This failure of social scientists to use their own insights into the nature of human interaction in their own methods of investigation has probably come through a drive to copy the methods of the natural scientists. As the social scientist investgates he is prepared to use the armoury of concepts that form the theoretical models of his subject and form a map in his mind into which he will fit his observations. Only some parts of the situation are noted. Psychologists will select different aspects from sociologists. Each part is fitted into his mental map. The rest is of peripheral interest to him as a scientist. What emerges in the account that is finally prepared is a pruned, synthetic version of the whole, a constructed play of puppet in a restricted environment.[7] Each social science produces its own type of puppet show within the contexts that are relevant to that discipline.

This is not a criticism of social science for not being concerned with real people in real situations. Scientific method depends on synthesising. The danger is that the constructed puppets may be mistaken for actual human actors. Social scientists are themselves often guilty of producing an ideal constructed type and later using it as if it were an actual description. But only through such simplified constructions can the complexity of human life be reduced to a pattern of related concepts that offer a chance of discovering relations and laws. The social scientist uses a simplified rational model of human behaviour in his pursuit of scientific detachment.

Schoeffler has dramatically analysed the failure of economists to escape from this dilemma of social science:

> They artificially mechanize, artificially simplify, artificially generalize, artificially fixate, artificially factorize, artificially close, artificially semiclose, and artificially isolate. They employ an artificial indirectness. They assume the heterogeneous to be homogeneous, the

complex to be simple, the complexly related to be simply related, the unknown to be known, the variable to be fixed, the open to be closed, the connected to be isolated and the indeterminate to be determinate.[8]

Cicourel has described researchers not as collectors of inert directly measurable facts, but as active interpreters of the events.[9] This interpretation involves both the use of language and of everyday meanings. In many cases it means interpreting what the subjects of the investigation meant, or what those who reported the behaviour of others meant. Just as the historian is necessarily involved in assessing the real meaning of documentary evidence from another age, so the social scientist is involved in sorting out the meaning of what has been seen, written or said. Both have to ask about the meaning to the persons being studied, to others who collected the information together and to themselves as they sort it out in a meaningful way. At each stage a person involved in one culture, one class, one period of time, may have to give meaning to words spoken or written in others.

Cicourel emphasises that it has been rare for social scientists to examine this stage of interpretation. But the crucial question is why was that meaning given to that act at that time and in that place. This is by no means a universally held view of priorities in social research, but it is less dangerous than the assumption that human behaviour is open to controlled scientific investigation. Reliability in social science can often only be achieved at the cost of validity. Interpretation can be excluded by rigid design of the investigation but in doing so any relevance to everyday life is likely to be lost.

This interaction between involvement and detachment is why there are no laws in the social sciences that have the universality of some in the natural sciences. Humans, whether as researchers or subjects, engage actively in the research process, reducing the extent of control. When a physicist observes the volume of a gas as the pressure exerted on it is altered with the temperature held constant, he can refer his observations to those of many others in a much repeated experiment. But the units for measuring volume, pressure and temperature are defined in advance and used by successive experimenters. As a scientist he uses definitions which relate his findings to those of innumerable other scientists. Furthermore, the limits of temperature and pressures within which the volume of a gas remains inversely proportional to the pressure exerted on it have also been determined by repeated experiment. The social scientist by contrast has often to prune or distort his observations to fit into his conceptual boxes. Some will just not fit, for the data is the product of human interaction, not scientific definition and control.

There is therefore a gap between the ambitious, abstract theorising of some social scientists and the modest data collected from numerous small-scale studies of concrete situations. Rarely do the latter illuminate the former. Indeed, it is unusual for the speculative theories about the human condition to be phrased in a way that could be verified through research. Frequently the concepts are so abstract that they could never be defined in a way that would enable their interrelation to be tested. Glaser and Strauss have seen the answer in grounded theory which is developed during, not in advance of, investigation.[10] This is an attack on speculation not theory, an attempt to give it substance, not to challenge its importance. Grounded theory is an attempt to bridge the gap that is the central concern of this book. It avoids the common divorce between abstract theorising and the evidence from actual investigation.

The danger of speculative theory developed in academic disciplines that are applied to concrete situations such as the classroom has been amusingly described by Holt[11] who has concentrated on the chasm between the theories on education and the actual experience of children in school. Holt has been primarily concerned with the reasons why children fail. But his work constitutes an incidental attack on educational research that is devastating, if naïve. To Holt, children develop complicated strategies for finding or stealing answers. When a question is asked they search for clues, not in the information supplied, but in the gestures, hints, tone of voice and behaviour of the teacher or questioner. The answers given are not the child's real views but his informed guess at the answer that the teacher or researcher wants him to give. If the researcher, like the teacher, has some speculative theory that loads his questions, the children are liable to give the answers that will verify it.

A further contrast that can be made between the natural and social sciences is the rarity of replication in the latter. A physicist can refer to gas laws, not because these hold under any conditions, but because the relation between the volume, pressure and temperature of a gas has been tested experimentally innumerable times under controlled conditions. This has not only established confidence in the relations but has determined the conditions within which they hold.

Replication in the social sciences is difficult because of the difficulty in controlling all the factors under investigation. Each occasion tends to be unique. Significantly, only experimental psychology, where controls under laboratory conditions can be imposed has established a reliable base by replication. But here the conditions are synthetic and generalisation to normal human behaviour perilous. It may also be that social scientists, like all pioneers, find the breaking of new ground more rewarding than the consolidation of existing territory. The nature of social scientific investigation also makes it difficult to employ students for replication as the work, far from being confined to the laboratory, spills out into the private lives of the public. Indeed, students are likely to be such an influential factor in the investigations in which they are involved that they would not really be replicating at all.

MODELS AND METHODS IN PSYCHOLOGY AND SOCIOLOGY

The models and maps in the minds of social scientists are derived from the theories that have been established within the separate disciplines. Here psychology and sociology have been selected to show the differences in perspective, but all the sciences concerned with human behaviour have their own distinctive stance. The importance of knowing at least the outline of the framework of concepts in a science is that the methods used in inquiry are not merely techniques but are intimately connected with their theoretical origins. Each subject is truly a discipline, imposing on those who practise it a perspective that determines their research procedures.

In this book the majority of examples are from sociology and that part of psychology which deals with social interaction. Every example should be referred back to the theoretical foundations at the base of the subject. Only this procedure can relate the methods used and the evidence produced to the models of human behaviour used by the researcher. In some cases research will have been undertaken without such a theoretical stance, but if it has not stopped at being a technical exercise there will have been reference to some theoretical model, however imperfectly defined this was in the mind of the researcher. It is not possible here to do more than crudely contrast two social sciences. The author is certainly not competent to do even this. No reader can be familiar with the variety of social sciences. Nevertheless a realisation that methods of inquiry and evidence are only fully comprehended through referral back to their theoretical origins is crucial.

It would be misleading, however, to imply that psychology and sociology are unified subjects. In practice each is split into many conflicting groups. Uneasy under the bedclothes of psychology are behaviourists obtaining their evidence from controlled experiments, and Freudians obtaining theirs from patients on the couch. While some sociologists try to match the natural sciences in technique and apparent detachment, others use the subject as a launching pad for what they see as an overdue attack on established social order. Indeed a major difference between the natural and social sciences is that the former try to keep their conflicts private while the latter slang one another in public.

Psychology is concerned with the study of the mental processes of individuals. Its basic concepts include learning, perception, emotion, motivation, thinking, personality and intelligence. These and others are related to each other to form the distinctive conceptual framework of the subject. These concepts are usually defined by reference to the behaviour through which they are manifested. The accompanying methods are concerned therefore with the measurement of that behaviour. This usually means that the behaviour is produced experimentally under controlled conditions. The trend in psychology has been from introspection to controlled experiment as the chief method of obtaining knowledge about individual mental processes.

Thus psychological inquiry is guided by the conceptual system that has been developed in the subject. The behaviour investigated, the methods chosen and the interpretation of results are all influenced by the theories relating the concepts into models of human behaviour. The focus, the methods and the evidence produced by inquiry are determined by the concern with individual mental processes. Even where social psychologists are investigating behaviour in groups, they refer back to individual behaviour for explanations.

Sociology is concerned with the interaction between social groups. The basic concepts, culture, social structure and role, are properties of groups. Sociologists are interested in individual behaviour, but as a way to establishing the roles that typify persons in particular positions within social groups. This interest usually rules out controlled experiment as a method. If groups are in focus their structure and working must not be distorted by the introduction of controls. Neither can information be gathered from individuals and be added together and assumed to illuminate properties of groups.

The methods used by sociologists are designed therefore to preserve group structure and normal operating. Observation and survey are basic and control has to be exercised through the comparison of similar groups in different environments. The comparative method is fundamental because it does not disturb everyday situations. The usual sociological theory is phrased as a relation between two factors such as social class and educational opportunity, or income and life style. But these relations are not established by controlling all other possible intervening factors, for this would either destroy the structure of the groups involved or require an impossibly large number of groups so that other intervening factors were randomised.

A sociologist would approach the family of spouses and mother-in-law with his focus on individuals to build up generalisations about husband, wife and her mother, the relations between them and the norms that govern these relationships. He may be further interested in the way areas of freedom are carved out by those involved. For explanations he would be looking at the total context of family life, at the way roles in society are defined and at the relation of the family and other institutions. He is not concerned with individual motives, emotions, or personalities, except where their study helps explain the patterns of interaction.

It woud be wrong to imply that psychologists always operate at the individual level while sociologists confine themselves to the collective. Examples where definition and procedure is at one level but analysis slips to another will be discussed in chapter 12. Psychologists have assumed they can generalise about groups when all they have is data on a number of individuals who in reality have nothing in common. Sociologists do collect information on groups and then stretch this to discuss individual behaviour. But such fallacies can be detected as evidence is being assessed. More difficult to cater for while gauging reliability and validity are the differences within each social science. Psychologists interested in measuring behaviour through testing in laboratory conditions are easily distinguishable from sociologists who see groups as having an existence that is not reducible to individual behaviour. But a major growth in sociology has been the concentration on the actor, the meaning he gives to his situation and the clues he manufactures for others. Similarly some psychologists concentrating on group behaviour deal with structure in the same way as sociologists. No single book or individual can fully plot this variety. The very terms psychology and sociology are examples of the ideal synthetic constructions that each uses. There is little resemblance to the variety actually found in each profession.

This situation of contrast and similarity between sociology and psychology is matched by other sciences concerned with human interaction. Each has its own synthetic models. The variety of subjects and models makes it difficult for the lay reader, or someone concerned with a borrowing subject such as education, to see what sort of straitjacket on the data is being applied by a writer. All that can be recognised is the relation between the evidence, the way it was obtained and the theoretical framework that determined the method of inquiry.

This situation of conflicts within subjects and contrasts between them makes it difficult for those who use the evidence of the social sciences to determine reliability and validity. Education particularly uses social scientific evidence *à la carte*, picking bits that seem useful rather than taking the whole offering. Thus evidence tends to be used without knowledge of the intentions of the chef about the whole meal, or the conditions in the kitchen.

DEFINITIONS

There are two difficulties in knowing what is meant by terms used in social science. The first arises out of the necessity of referring words back to their origins within specific subject disciplines. The second comes from the everyday source and everyday use of terms also used technically within the social sciences. Controversy 1 (p. 28) should be read with these two difficulties in mind.

The difficulty in establishing what is really meant by a term is increased by the simultaneous use of the same terms in two or more disciplines, yet with subtle, crucial changes of meaning. Thus Swift has argued that psychologists have borrowed the term 'environment' from sociology, yet used it in a way that ignores the essence of the term when it is used to explain individual behaviour.[12] To a sociologist the crucial part of the environment is not physical conditions but the means through which social experiences influence a person's perspective of the world. Individuals make sense of their environment through their interaction with others. They learn as they are involved in social processes. The psychologist sees the environment much as he sees a maze in which he is running his rats, as a set of physical barriers. Thus the psychologist establishes measures of physical conditions and uses these as indices of the environment. But these measures may be sociologically irrelevant.

There is a further complication in this borrowing. Swift and Acland have pointed to the tendency of psychologists to divorce sociological variables such as environment or social group from the theories which have given them meaning, in order to measure them by the typical psychological method approximating to the controlled experiment.[13] Unfortunately, matching delinquents with non-delinquents, or those from one area with those from another, results in analysis in terms of individuals. The sociologist is concerned with the organisation of groups, their norms and the effects of group membership on the individuals who belong to them. Matched samples of individuals are likely to have nothing in common and comparisons between them can throw no light on the influence of genuine social groups or their environment.

Swift has been careful to point out that sociologists are as guilty of this careless borrowing as psychologists. The two subjects operate at different levels and terms defined at the social level can not be used to analyse data collected from individuals.[14] Neither can psychological terms developed within a theoretical framework referring to individual characteristics be used to throw light on information collected from the observation of groups. Individuals have their properties and groups have theirs. Definitions have meaning only within a body of theory we call a discipline. The same word may mean different things in different disciplines. The fallacies which may result through differences in the levels of theory and data collection are discussed in chapter 10.

The second problem over the definition of words arises out of the way social scientists base their constructs on the existing everyday constructs made by those under investigation. The desire to understand real situations involves a search for words that summarise and clarify often muddled everyday activity. The desire to communicate this understanding limits the social scientist to the use of adaptations of everyday language. But these words have a meaning imposed on them through the discipline involved. The same word describing some crucial concept may have a common meaning, a specific meaning to the investigating scientist but another specific meaning to a scientist from another discipline.

In practice the situation is even more confused. In addition to the lay meaning and the abstraction from it to fit some specific framework of concepts there is a third level of operational definition. This is used once the scientist tries to observe, measure and classify. It is a definition in terms of the operations that are about to be performed. Thus in the controversy that follows, intelligence is often used operationally as that which is measured by intelligence tests. Social class is usually operationally defined by father's occupation.

These operational definitions lie behind statistics. They are serving as indices of some concept. But the fit between index and concept may be imperfect. Intelligence and social class are not usually used in the sense outlined above. Such a definition facilitates measurement but may give little valid information on the concept under review. Above all, concepts such as suburb or teacher effectiveness, while easy to translate into some measurable term are liable to be translated into new ones every time they are investigated. The consequence has been a mass of data but nothing that has served to accumulate knowledge. Each piece of research stands isolated and comparisons are difficult.

The existence of three levels of definition also leads to slipping from one to another. The controversy over the relation between racial differences and the distribution of intelligence that follows has been rich in experiment but rife with switches of level, so that the protagonists rarely argue about the same definition of race or intelligence. Indeed, all the controversies in this book should be interpreted in this way. There is much shadow boxing in social science, for the reasonable desire to get involved in big issues is rarely matched by research that can do more than suggest indices. Issue and index may lie far apart.

It is not only that words are used without agreed definition but that some are assumed to need none. 'Society' appears frequently but is rarely defined. This could be merely pedantic, but 'society' can be used as if it had concrete reality divorced from the individuals within it. Societies are said to exert pressure, to be served by organisations, to have characters. At its worst this can result in terms like collective consciousness or general will, which are absurd until defined and they disappear with definition.

It is too easy to draw conclusions about issues that have never been initially defined. The clarification of the meaning of words has rightly been a major concern of modern philosophy. In social science the perilous terms are the ones that sound convincing. Delinquent subculture, cultural deprivation, activity methods or social background carry with them some aura of reliability. Yet definition in these areas has been so weak that replication has been difficult and each has been replaced by more precise and less global terms. The lay reader is entitled to suspect the use of jargon just as the professional can legitimately criticise slippery or absent definitions.

Child development studies are a prime example of the soapy use of terms. Play, love, conscience, imitation have been used in many ways by different writers but have rarely been spelled out. A typical case has been the influential theory of maternal deprivation associated with the work of Bowlby.[15] Wootton, examining this hypothesis that the separation of the child from the mother in infancy, or the loss of the mother's affection determines the child's ability to form stable personal relations, has listed the numerous definitions in use.[16] So loosely defined is the hypothesis that the evidence for and against is equally unsuitable as a basis for determining the extent, incidence and causes of disturbance through deprivation. Replications of Bowlby's work have produced nothing about the critical conditions of deprivation, the extent and persistence of emotional disturbance, or of the relation between them.[17]

This research has been very influential. It showed that current practice in British children's hospitals and homes, involving the separation of young children from their parents, was doing harm. On the other hand it may have stopped the setting up of social services in developing countries which would have enabled women to go out to work. The practical influence of research is probably unrelated to its reliability.

The clarity of definition in natural science is part of the control exercised. A term like 'absolute temperature' may bewilder the public, but this point where molecular activity is assumed to cease enables physicists to use one another's results with confidence. In social science such precision is rarely possible. But it is also rarely desirable. Where the aim is understanding, precision often has to be sacrificed. Significantly, experimental psychology which has gone furthest among the social sciences in using controlled experimentation and consequently replication studies has been most criticised for producing a lot about the useless. The evidence may be reliable but because of the controls exercised it tells us little about human behaviour. In anthropology, at the other extreme, there is pressure to be naïve to preserve an open mind in the field, but a realisation that this naïvety limits the scope of the conclusions that can be made.[18]

Controversy 1
Should scientists investigate sensitive social problems?

The conventional view of science is of detached pursuit of knowledge. In practice, the personal involvement of the scientist in the issues he investigates increases as they become of pressing public concern. It is not just that the scientist will be exposed to personal as well as professional criticism, but that attacks on his personal motives for undertaking the work will be extended to challenge his competence as a scientist.

In 1969 Jensen reviewed the literature on racial and social class differences in intelligence.[1] This was followed by another issue of the *Harvard Educational Review* devoted to critiques of his views[2] and a further issue containing his replies to his critics.[3] With the explosive racial situation in the U.S.A., Jensen's suggestion that there were innate differences in the distribution of measured intelligence between races was sure to cause an uproar. But three points stand out in the ensuing dispute. First, many thought the subject should never have been investigated. Second, there were vitriolic attacks on the personal integrity of Jensen. Third, his standing as a psychologist was challenged. Similar criticisms were later made of his supporters in Britain.

The Jensen report was used by segregationists in the Southern States of the U.S.A. to justify existing inequalities in education.[4] Jensen, however, maintained that he was trying to develop a new theory of intelligence that would hold more hope for successful compensatory education, thus helping ethnic minorities. Brazziel, however, claimed that the *Harvard Educational Review* had acted irresponsibly in publishing evidence that would inevitably be misunderstood and used to sustain inequality.[5] Another critic maintained that to raise the issue at all was racism.[6]

In this dispute personal abuse was mixed with academic criticism. Jensen was likened to Governor Wallace, was accused of supporting the idea of Negro inferiority and of justifying school segregation.[7] When the National Foundation for Educational Research decided to include an article by Jensen in *Educational Research* it was attacked for its racialist content, but also for the pseudo-scientific nature of the evidence produced even before the actual article was published[8]. The validity of the evidence was challenged in advance. The National Foundation was accused of "elevating a bogus and largely discredited thesis into respectibility".[9] The acting director of the National Foundation replied that it would have been prejudice and censorship not to publish a contribution from such a distinguished psychologist.[10]

More fuel had been added to this dispute by the publication in Britain of a book by Eysenck before the furore over the original Jensen article had died down.[11] Here a serious social and academic issue was virtually reduced to farce by the conflicting critics.[12] The author, a refugee from Hitler's Europe, was accused of Fascism. Methodological errors bordering on lunacy were suggested and terms like ignorant and impudent abounded. Eysenck was accused of playing into the hands of politicians, of disregarding the work of environmentalists and of being unscientific and unscholarly. Unfortunately this apparent incompetence was seen to be combined with an effortless, masterly and persuasive style that would too easily capture the imagination of the intelligent plain man.[13] Academic incompetence, a lack of personal integrity and a facility to seduce the public were seen as combined.

The only way the plain man can cut through this animosity is to wait until the original controversy has died down. Thus Bodmer and Cavalli-Sforza in a calm review of the evidence over a year after the publications of Jensen's original article concluded that the currently available evidence was inadequate to resolve the question in either direction.[14] They agree that in the present climate of opinion the chances of misinterpretation of the evidence are so high that publication inevitably increased racial tensions. Above all they saw many more useful biological problems for the scientist to tackle that could lead to more conclusive answers and more fruitful action.

, This balanced view contrasts with the emotion generated earlier. First, there is no accusation of stupidity, personal malice or political reaction. When controversial subjects are investigated the scientist runs the risk of being labelled not only as a Fascist or a Communist, but as an imbecile. Second, the priority given to the research is judged against alternative possibilities, not against the political climate. The danger of accusing publishers of airing disruptive views is that it can lead to censorship. The liberal critics of Jensen and Eysenck were themselves under attack from more radical social scientists who saw the need, not to stop at criticism, but to convert social science into action against an unfair situation.[15] With such diverse views the struggle might focus on who had the right to censor, not on the quality of the articles presented for publication.

Perhaps the most alarming aspect of this controversy was its value as news. It was reported in newspapers and popular magazines as well as academic journals. In all there was some discussion of the reliability of the methods used in collecting the evidence. This unusual concern with reliability occurs only when accepted views are challenged. It acts as another pressure on the scientist when choosing his research area. When the reward may be recognition by some colleagues and the hatred of others; when personal integrity, political belief and professional competence are likely to be discussed in public, and when brief, often distorted versions are to reappear through the mass media, the scientist is no longer a detached observer. It is a brave man who will expose his work to both the microscope and the hatchet.

Questions of author, subject and date 3

An accused man is assumed innocent until proved guilty. This legal basis for assessment decreases the chances of injustice. Because an author chooses to put his views before the public he can justifiably be assumed guilty of bias until he shows that he is innocent. In some cases there is no difficulty in detecting a onesided selection of information or an expression of opinion that ignores the existence of evidence. In other cases it is clear that the author is sticking close to the evidence that he or others have collected. In between, the majority of books and articles contain evidence that has been selected and organised to argue a case. It is here that the reader needs to look for clues about the possible ways in which the beliefs of the author have determined the picture presented.

Authors have a variety of motives for writing. They have in common only a desire to spread information, exert influence and gain material rewards or prestige. The first major distinction is between books and articles that are attempts to produce reliable evidence and those that reflect only the views of the author. The presence of references to research results is no guarantee of objectivity. Flat-earthers have no difficulty accumulating convincing evidence. Lunatic theories of human behaviour are even easier to support by dependable looking evidence.

A further distinction has to be made between books and articles in popular journals such as *New Society* or *Forum* and research papers published in journals for professionals such as the *British Journal of Psychology* or *Sociology*. Not only does the technical level of these articles differ, but so do the motives of the authors.

Books and popular articles tend to be written as collections of work that has already appeared in professional journals. The writer of a book is paid by the publisher. In the social, as in the natural sciences, prestige is as likely to be lost as much as gained through the effort at reaching a wide audience. Whereas a research paper for fellow professionals is designed to advance existing knowledge about events or techniques, and must include sufficient description of methods to enable the readers to assess its reliability, a book or popular article tends to include only enough method to indicate how the information was obtained. Finally, fellow professionals are assumed to have read the literature relevant to the subject and all that is required is the shorthand of a few references. But a book or popular article has to summarise and simplify this background material.

A most alarming development is the proliferation of 'readers' presenting extracts from a number of sources on a subject. Another is the production of simple, filleted versions for students or symposia as in controversy 2. These present the core of the original without any accompanying description of methods and their shortcomings which appear in the original. No opportunity or invitation is given to assess reliability or validity. Students and public fed on a diet of readers and popular accounts would have little idea of the real nature of social science.

THE DATE OF PUBLICATION

In the 1970 general election in Britain the failure of the pollsters was proportional to the span of time which elapsed between the last survey and election day.[1] Opinion Research Centre was nearest the actual result and completed its fieldwork last. Marplan was farthest out and completed its fieldwork soonest. It is rare for a few days to make such a difference, but there is always a need to consider the year in which a work was published. This stems partly from the accumulation of books on library shelves and on book lists, and partly from the mechanics of writing and publishing. Books are removed to reserve stacks of libraries because of shortage of shelf space rather than redundancy. Book lists supplied to students tend to be antiquated not only through infrequent amendment, but the tendency of tutors to keep recommending books which they possess and have found useful in the past, or even written themselves. This combination of academic inertia, sentimentality and even greed results in a need to examine the date of publication in relation to developments within subject disciplines.

An examination of the book lists in *Education* given to students in four colleges and two departments of education in 1969 revealed several books, excellent in themselves, which seem to have survived beyond the system they were describing. Four of the five books on the English Educational System included in all lists were over ten years old, two having been published in 1955, one in 1957 and the other in 1949, revised in 1952. While excellent, all were written before major changes in central administration and before the development on a large scale of new forms of secondary and further education. In educational psychology the most frequently recommended book was published in 1956. The most frequently recommended book on child development was based on Susan Isaacs's work at Malting House School between 1924 and 1927 and on Charlotte Buhler's work in Vienna in the 1920s.[2] All the lists included the study by Floud, Halsey and Martin on *Social Class and Educational Opportunity* published in 1956.[3] These works have survived because they have become classics, but the normal child of one decade may be abnormal in the next, and descriptions of contemporary adminstration become history with each change in legislation.

Ageing is not the only danger. Books are reprinted frequently, particularly in paperback, but revised rarely. A glance through the dates of reprints to the last date of revision or original date of publication is particularly necessary in popular books. Furthermore, publishing is a slow process. There is often an eighteen-month delay between an article for an academic journal in the social sciences being accepted and its publication. A book takes a similar time to produce from the acceptance of the typescript.

A glance at the preface will often give the date of completion by the author which is usually at least a year before the date of publication. Some academic journals give the date when the typescript was received.

In the type of article or book considered here there is a further complication. The evidence on which they have been based may have been collected long before the work was published. Books are often adapted from higher degree theses or from articles based on field work done in the past. A further step, therefore, is to find out when the evidence was collected. Thus books on child development still draw on work done in the 1920s. Hemming's study of *Problems of Adolescent Girls* was published in 1960, but based on letters written to a magazine between 1953 and 1955.[4] Tapper's study of political socialisation, *Young People and Society* was published in 1971 with the Labour Party in opposition, and based on information collected just after the defeat of the Conservative Party in 1964.[5] The transition from hard to soft cover is also slow. The study by Hargreaves of *Social Relations in a Secondary School* was published as hardback in 1967 and paperback in 1970.[6] The fieldwork was done in 1963 and 1964. By the time three follow-up studies directed by J. W. B. Douglas dealing with children under five,[7] primary schooling,[8] and experience up to school leaving or the threshold of the sixth form[9] were published, their subjects had reached the ages respectively of twelve, eighteen and twenty-two. It must be remembered that these books are among the most reliable as they do include and describe the sources of their evidence. Where this is missing, the reader is left to guess how relevant the information still is.

A rare example of clear presentation of the historical development of a research project which also is refreshingly free of didactic deadpan is the published account of the work of the Sociological Research Unit.[10] Here the attempts to obtain finance in 1962, final success and start in 1964 through to finish at Christmas 1967 are described. Significantly, this monograph, published in 1970, also includes reports of breakdowns, changes of direction and warnings of possible unreliability.

Another reason for watching the date of publication refers to the redundancy of words rather than events. Social change is accompanied by changes in the meanings of words. To call someone liberal, gay or high may be complimentary one year but insulting the next. Jewish in 1939 indicated pacific and defensive. In 1970 it implied militant and aggressive. In education the term secondary used to mean the selective school before 1944, but non-selective as well thereafter. A technical college no longer means primarily evening classes, but a variety of mainly daytime courses. Scripture becomes religious instruction and then religious education. But these are only the obvious changes. Words are part of a continually changing set of symbols employed by men to communicate. The changes are as subtle but as persistent as the changes in the life the words express. An author assumes that his words can bring a picture to the reader's mind. But once time has passed the same word may produce a different picture. Yesterday's survey becomes history. Yesterday's words refer to a different world.

It is also advisable to determine the audience for whom the book was written and the place where the evidence was collected. Psychology and sociology still tend to be dominated by American texts. Yet in these, and subjects like education, it may be misleading to draw conclusions about British organisations and social relations from American experience. Again the crucial area is the collection of evidence. It should be noted in advance if the children whose development has been used for illustration were Viennese or American, that the educational system, social background, economy, history, language or politics are alien and therefore that generalisations may be misleading.

E. H. Carr has argued that this perspective can be illustrated from the study of history where it is necessary to study first the historical and social environment of the historian, then to investigate the bees that are buzzing under this particular historian's bonnet.[11] Only then can the reader have any idea of why the material designated as facts in the work came to be selected. Thus the facts of history are continually being amended as the context within which the historian works itself changes.

35

It is usually only a matter of time before accepted facts and theories are challenged. This is partly because such a challenge is a sure path to fame for the hatchet man. It is also due to changing political climates. It is not only in Soviet Russia that history is rewritten to match contemporary political alignments. In a slower, less brutal way it is continually happening through academic scepticism. An apparently obvious belief that the 1870 Education Act filled the gaps left by private provision in elementary education has persisted since it was used by Forster in introducing the Act. Intervention by the state was seen as essential to complete a system of popular schooling. West supporting the case for more private enterprise that was gaining force in the mid 1960s, launched an attack, not only on the need for state intervention at all, but on the way the available evidence had been used to convey a false impression of the failure of private initiative.[12] West's interpretation of the nineteenth-century statistics on education suggests that historians have been guilty ever since of accepting figures that were based only on schools subsidised by the state and which ignored the proliferating private schools which were neither subsidised nor inspected. Other writers, commenting on West's re-analysis, tend to agree that the state jumped on to a galloping horse in 1870 rather than lashing a reluctant beast into motion.[13]

Similar reinterpretations can be found in all subjects. In education, which uses many disciplines, the same procedure as in reading history is advisable. Books written before 1950 usually assumed that intelligence tests measured innate ability and that there were types of children that could be identified and given a schooling suitable for their aptitudes. A good index of the change since 1950 due to advances in psychological research is the derision heaped on the Norwood Report of 1941 and on the tripartite secondary schooling which this report seemed to support. Similarly, books written before 1960 tended to assume that waste of talent could be eliminated by the provision of better schools and facilities. By 1970 this was seen as naïve, and the focus had shifted to studying sources of motivation and deprivation in family and community, and resources were increasingly being devoted to improving the environment of schooling.

The speed of educational change makes it difficult to detect these changes from books and few can follow the accounts of research in academic journals. Hence there is a lag in new perspectives reaching the non-specialist reader and a danger that even a book written in the last decade may be misleading. An examination of reading lists for students on education courses will show many such cases. Thus two popular anthropological studies in paperback by Margaret Mead, *Coming of Age in Samoa*, published in 1929, and *Growing Up in New Guinea*, published in 1931, appear on most lists.[14] In both cases there remain paperback editions still being printed. These books may never have been accepted by professional anthropologists but are widely used to illustrate that patterns of upbringing differ between cultures and that it is possible for children to move smoothly through adolescence without much discipline and without emotional disturbance. Yet later writers have shown that it is easy for Western anthropologists to miss the real discipline of life in an apparently easygoing, simple society.[15] Generations of students have obtained a picture of life under the palms that would probably by unrecognisable to those actually lying there.

A final example from criminology will illustrate the same point that rapid advances in subject knowledge leave a residue on bookshelves that is misleading. The main historical interest in criminology has been in the reasons why laws were broken. This focused attention largely on working class youth. The first refocusing came in 1940 when Sutherland published his study of white collar crime and showed that it was the definition of what constituted a crime that mattered.[16] Much of contemporary criminology has developed this idea so that the focus is on why particular actions by particular groups of persons are labelled at particular times as crimes, rather than on why unchanging and agreed standards of behaviour are violated. Crime is seen as an interaction between groups in which those with power label some actions of those without as criminal.[17]

PRESSURES ON THE AUTHOR

Authors and researchers are subject to a variety of pressures as they select, plan, implement and report their work. The mildest yet most widespread in the social sciences is that involvement during research reduces detachment and the intricacies, idiosyncrasies, loves and hates of those studied come to be appreciated. Social scientists visiting schools, hospitals or factories for a brief visit and the quick application of an interview programme or questionnaire tend to give a cold, clinical and usually critical account. Participant observers come to see the difficulties faced by the teachers, the nurses or the workers. Their reports tend to be warm and any criticism is tempered by allowances due to adverse conditions. This is a crude generalisation, but it is important to look at the extent to which the writer involved himself and got interested in the human problems as well as the working efficiency of his subjects.

Authors are, however, often pressing a cause and their bias may not be eliminated by the research design. In education there are pressure groups supporting comprehensive schools, public schools, streaming and de-streaming. These groups are vocal, organised and eager to produce results that will support their case. The obvious clues are to be found in the publishers or sponsoring bodies. Political parties and societies, religious organisations and pressure groups publish or sponsor useful but slanted books and pamphlets. This information is often on the title page or in the preface. It is worth while to get to know the views of some of the associations with the largest output. Thus the Fabian Society in supporting the collective solution to social problems and the Institute of Economic Affairs in its support for private enterprise are pressing particular political beliefs though they may claim only to approve publications and not to influence the authors. The *Critical Quarterly* and the *New-Left Review* find no difficulty in accumulating evidence to support their conflicting cases.

Even where there are no obvious sources of bias, there is still a need to study the professional and social pressures on the author.

No scientist can escape these pressures, for the natural sciences require increasingly large sums of money and this tends to deflect research into channels approved by government or industry. A mass spectrometer, a basic instrument in a modern chemistry laboratory, costs around £30,000. Particle accelerators cost hundreds of million pounds. This type of money has to be obtained through bargaining. Many eminent American social scientists joined Project Camelot after it received 6 million dollars from the U.S. Army.[18] This was later terminated by the President of the United States when its objectives and political implications became suspect. Among the motives for joining was the attraction of belonging to a wealthy project close to the centre of power, a hope that the U.S. Army could be humanised and deflected into constructive work, and even an honest admission that the money was good. But the cost of association was the taint of involvement in a project which was concerned with uncovering data on the causes of revolutions, for use by the U.S. Army.

A more important restraint comes through controls exercised over individuals by the discipline of their subject. Undergraduate and graduate education immerses the student in books, lectures, tutorials and research procedures that are chosen and controlled by teaching or supervisory staff. Getting a place and a grant for a second degree or to do research usually means fitting in to the field of interests of existing faculty members. Getting an article published depends on the attitudes of established men who act as editors or referees. In this way each subject exerts control over its members and it becomes a discipline. Hagstrom has argued that within scientific communities in the natural sciences any disputes that do arise are limited by the actions of those controlling publicity, so that the majority remain working in areas where there is agreement and students are given an image of unified content and procedures.[19]

Some ideas of the conventions governing science can be gauged from Merton's view that the stress in science on advancing knowledge puts a premium on original contribution.[20] Rewards go to those who discover first, not only in the form of Nobel prizes, but through giving a name to a substance or process, thus bestowing immortality on men like Boyle, Mendel, Pavlov and Zeigarnik. This emphasis on originality often clashes with the other main stress in science on organised scepticism and objectivity. For most scientists, getting into print is a sufficient reward, symbolising originality, even if the reality was a routine report. The urge to publish is a result of the pressure on scientists to prove their ability to produce original ideas. The nearer to the frontiers of knowledge a scientist works, the greater is the pressure to succeed and the vulnerability of the individual to failure. The involvement of scientists with their peers is therefore a source of tension as well as of support.

Authors also write books from a viewpoint that is inevitably coloured by their own political ideology. An account by I.L. Horowitz of his reasons for writing *Revolution in Brazil* shows how the honest social scientist recognises this.[21] Horowitz was anxious to write a book about Brazil that did not contain the bias of many that had gone before. His own liberal view, transcending a purely nationalist perspective, led him to concentrate on areas of Brazilian life that had been of little interest before. But this was nevertheless a selection, honestly admitted to be a reflection of his own political views. A rare English example is Ford's expression of her socialism and hopes for an end to the system of stratification in Britain in her preface to her book *Social Class and the Comprehensive School*.[22]

The source of funds may also be an important influence on research. Sjoberg and many others have argued that major projects in American social science are prone to be influenced by the administration that sponsors the research, particularly where these sponsoring bodies are interested in maintaining social order. Thus Project Camelot, lavishly supported by the U.S. Army, was a study of the preconditions of internal conflict in Latin America and elsewhere. The social scientists had no apparent control over their work. Their critics have detected a stress on studying factors concerned with maintaining order so that the project seemed to some to be a study in counterinsurgency only.[23]

For most of human history thinkers who have supported

unpopular views have been silenced by those in authority over intellectual life. The worst modern example occurred in Soviet Russia under Stalin. From 1929 bourgeois elements in science were under attack. In 1936 the Medico-Genetical Institute was attacked in *Pravda* and then closed. In 1937 Lysenko, with support from Stalin, branded his opponents as deviationists and his own theories replaced classical, Mendelian genetics. Leading opponents were arrested and Vavilov the leading Russian geneticist was arrested, sentenced to death and actually died in prison in 1942, the year he was elected to the Royal Society.

The final triumph of Lysenko came in 1948, when hundreds of scientists were dismissed from their posts, had their degrees removed, were shadowed by the secret police and arrested. Books were removed from libraries and all teaching of Mendelism banned. From 1948 to 1952 Lysenko was supreme in Russian biology.[24] He was the only scientist to be called great in his lifetime. At his first lecture at the Agricultural Academy, staff as well as students attended. A brass band played as he went to the rostrum. The State Chorus had a hymn honouring him.

During this period discoveries abounded. They became increasingly absurd, but the support of Stalin and then Khrushchev was sufficient to silence critics. However, from 1952 a counter-attack developed. At first it concentrated on detail without openly criticising Lysenko. But the damage done to Russian agriculture finally weakened Lysenko's grip on Soviet science until attempts were made to affect a compromise with classical genetics. By 1963 open attacks were appearing and the advances of Western biology could no longer be concealed. Khrushchev resigned in 1964 and Lysenko was dismissed in 1965.

The lessons of the Lysenko tragedy support the case for continuous scepticism in science as well as continuous replication to test claims. A combination of circumstances helped Lysenko attain power over more distinguished scientists. His claims seemed to offer practical solutions to Russia's problems in agriculture. He was able to align his theories with the current political ideology and obtain the support of Stalin and Khrushchev. By branding his opponents as deviationists, spies and saboteurs he clawed his way above them. In a centralised scientific community all training could be rapidly adjusted to the new doctrine.

Nevertheless, it was not just the ability of the secret police to silence opposition that accounted for this triumph of pseudo-science. Under the conditions in a dictatorship that maintained that its ideology was itself scientific, the sceptic was a heretic to be liquidated. The claim of the Russian leaders that Marxism as interpreted by them contained the key to all problems, including those tackled by scientists, meant there could be no dispute allowed with the official Party line. The grip was tightened by centralised control over all the possible means whereby critics could publicise their views. Furthermore, potential critics were isolated from the community of international scientists who might have supported them. It was not only biology that suffered from the political accusations of the Party leaders, but also the other natural sciences and all those subjects that study man which were flourishing elsewhere during this period.

The Lysenko case is an extreme example of the interference of government in science; similar, if less extreme, cases could be found in the witch-hunting during the McCarthy era in the United States in the first half of the 1950s. Once the direction of scientific activity is dictated from outside the scientific community, and once the allegiance of scientists is to governments, a source of scientific reliability is sacrificed. The drive of individual scientists to get the recognition of their fellows and the granting of this recognition only after agreement has been reached about evidence by established scientists may have undesirable effects, but does guarantee that fraud is unlikely to pass and that professional competence will be required before acceptance is accorded.

It is not only in totalitarian regimes that scientific activity has been controlled for political purposes. American and British scientists have lost their jobs because of their political beliefs. In 1970 there was a typical example of the suppression of a report attacking the established policies of a scientific community. A long discussion paper prepared by Huberman for Unesco was ordered to be destroyed by the Director General.[25] From surviving copies it is evident than this destruction was aimed to stop the circulation of a swingeing attack on the conventional policies of this agency and in education generally. Such book-burning has occurred periodically in history in a variety of different religious and political climates. Less obvious, but more general pressures come from colleagues, editors, censors and organisations providing the money for research. Furthermore, the public listens to, and buys, what it wants to hear and read. It is easy to pander to this self-satisfying taste and inhibit the distasteful and unpopular. The published is always selected.

Individual scientists are not only influenced by state policy and the views of agencies providing the money, but by their own personal ambition. Robert Hooke, a prolific inventor was forever contesting with men like Newton and Huygens about who had invented things first. Cavendish, Watt and Lavoisier all claimed to have first demonstrated the compound nature of water. Sir Humphry Davy opposed the election of Michael Faraday to the Royal Society because he maintained that Faraday's discovery of electromagnetic rotation was not original.

A remarkable illustration of the mixture of personal ambition, determination to beat rivals and scientific inventiveness has been provided by Watson's account of his work with Crick on the structure of the D.N.A. molecule.[26] The book also demonstrates how an author unconsciously puts himself at the centre of events and of the creative process. The search for a model of this molecule that would satisfy existing knowledge was being sought in many places. Crick and Watson felt the pressure of competition as they neared their solution and feared that one of the other groups concerned would come up with a successful solution first. The discovery was seen as one which would qualify for a Nobel prize. While this account probably leaves out the more mundane work and the real expertise of those concerned, it is a startling revelation of the motivation of scientists working around the frontiers of knowledge.

The scientist is therefore under pressure to establish his prior claim. As a consequence it is usual in the journals of natural sciences to publish the date of receiving manuscripts. This is the case with most journals of psychology but unusual in sociology or education. The relation between originality and recognition also appears in the tendency to use the number of publications as a measure of accomplishment. The urge to publish and the recognition of genuine originality are part of the same tradition, though they may have little else in common.

There are rare instances where personal ambition seems to have led to fraud. The history of science is littered with deliberate deceptions and sincere fallacies, and the line between the two has often been difficult to draw. One of the most famous cases of this type was the discovery in 1911 of the Dawn Man of Piltdown by the amateur geologist and archaeologist Charles Dawson.[27] The support of Arthur Smith Woodward, a noted scientist, overcame most of the contemporary doubts about the reliability of the evidence. Although the remains did not fit in with other contemporary evidence and were to stay isolated phenomena the few doubters were not listened to. In 1913 digging and sieving exposed other remains and in 1915 Dawson found more remains of a second Piltdown man. The anticipated evidence of man's ape-like ancestry seemed to have been found. Dawson died in 1916 and no further remains were found. *Eoanthropus dawsoni* existed as an anomaly. By 1948 new techniques had showed that the Piltdown skull was not more than 50,000 years old. Next, parts of the skull were shown to be of different ages and constitution. Then staining was detected and the teeth were shown to have been filed down. The jaw was shown to be that of an orang utan. Implements found near the skull were shown to have been recently shaped and stained and most of the fossils found nearby were frauds. This was a forgery that had been the work of a professional, skilled enough to convince some of the most august scientists of the time. It may have been an elaborate joke, an attempt to obtain fame or a deliberate fraud. The important point is that such evidence had been expected and was sufficient to convince not only the public, but leading scientists of the time.

The allocation of resources for research is also determined by factors which may have no relation to the usefulness of the subject. The funds available and the attraction of researchers to a particular field are often decided without regard to the utility of the possible outcome of the work. Thus the autonomy of the universities determined that the committee under Lord Robbins set up to examine higher education was appointed under a Treasury minute by the Prime Minister.[28] All the other major reports on education have been produced by committees of the Central Advisory Council for Education, working in areas suggested by the Minister of Education. It is perhaps symbolic of this difference that the report on higher education for a small minority cost £129,000, whereas the Newsom Report, *Half our Future*, also published in 1963, only cost £13,000.[29]

Social and political influences bear on the author and researcher through his involvement in a profession and directly. The subjects that are taught in an academic department and the resources allocated to research are determined by decisions about finance made outside as well as inside the faculty. An individual is appointed for teaching or research because his interests and skills fit into the pattern of the department. He becomes part of a group concentrating on specific areas of study, themselves often determined by the allocation of funds on the basis of such factors as economic usefulness or political expediency. In the social sciences the individual is prone to be involved in departmental interests in problems seen as relevant to contemporary society. Once geared to this subject interest, however, change is slow and inertia keeps resources flowing into the study of redundant issues. Consequently there tends to be a concentration of books and articles in particular subjects on narrow issues that may have lost their relevance for the lay reader, while more important issues are neglected. The consequence is that books on crucial contemporary issues are often written by non-specialists lacking adequate resources, while those with facilities for research and with the support of academic departments continue to work on topics that are of little interest to the non-academic reader.

In both the natural and social sciences energy has been wasted. Great effort has gone into proving the obvious and probing the trivial. The commitment of scientists to their community can blind them to the futility of their work. But where the alchemist could waste little but his own time, modern scientific enterprises can absorb fortunes. Project Mohole seems to have started as a way of boosting the prestige of the earth sciences.[30] It was established as part of AMSOC, the American Miscellaneous Society, which had been founded as a comic contrast to established scientific societies. The object was to bore a hole deep into the earth's crust. But accurate costing, specific objectives and sound organisation were neglected amid professional envy and political chicanery. Estimates rocketed from 5 to 125 million dollars. In the end the project was stopped by Act of Congress in 1966. Significantly, this action followed articles in journals reporting science to the public in an intelligible way. Science, secure within communities can easily obscure its shortcomings from the public.

Controversy 2
Can young children make transitive inferences?

This controversy links the preceding chapters on the way research is reported to the public with the technical chapters that follow. It is concerned with the use made of the work of Piaget rather than with the work itself. If the sign of good theory is the number of hypotheses and investigations it generates, then Piaget occupies the central place in developmental psychology. The frequency with which his work has been translated, simplified and adapted for guiding policy in education is another indication of his importance. Yet Piaget has shown little interest in classroom practices. The application of his learning theories to educational practice has been the work of others.

To obtain a clue to the weight placed on Piaget's theories in the 1960s requires an historical study of the work itself. He was born in 1896 and is still active. He writes in an obscure style, requiring not only translation into English but simplification and interpretation for understanding by a wide audience. One sympathetic writer has likened his writing to the Bible in its capacity for misinterpretation.[1] Piaget's research reports contain few clues on the actual methods used. Finally the experiments form only a part of a massive theory of child development that is still being developed and which is woven into Piaget's philosophical and sociological work. When the writing of such an original, obscure and encyclopaedic thinker is adapted by others for use in solving problems for which it was not intended, controversy is inevitable.

The need to interpret and evaluate Piaget for teachers has meant that once experiments that were often only loosely controlled have been replicated and shown to be unreliable there comes a need for reassessment and reinterpretation. But the result of such failures to replicate is also to indulge in what is now called Piaget bashing. An example of this occurred in 1971. Part of Piaget's learning theory was that children under seven could not make abstract inferences of the "if A is greater than B, and B is greater than C, then A must be greater than C" type. This has been an important influence on teaching in the infant school. Yet replications of Piaget's experiments by Bryant and Trabasso have shown that such transitive inferences can be made by children under seven, once the design of Piaget's original experiment is altered.[2] Other work on concept formation in young children has confirmed that Piaget had probably used methods that were too open to his own personal interpretations of what he observed.[3] Indeed, it has been argued that children are so skilled at detecting clues in such experiments that they will be merely reflecting back the results that the researcher hopes will emerge.[4]

However, it is in the popular reporting of such failures to replicate that the gap between scientific paper and public version can be seen. Piaget's supporters have maintained that he has argued that his work is not sufficiently thorough to serve as a basis for a scientific pedagogy.[5] Yet the Press seized on the Bryant and Trabasso replications and headlines in the *Observer* of "Children scupper Piaget's Law" were followed elsewhere by reports of Piaget's theory being undermined and by forecasts of major changes in teaching methods.[6] The *Daily Telegraph*, after reporting that the educational world would never be the same again, went on to predict that primary school teachers could now get down to teaching rather than minding fun parties.[7] These reports, in line with the political leanings of the papers concerned, turned out to be based on a telephone call from an *Observer* reporter to Bryant.[8] Inevitably there was dispute over what he actually said when he complained that he had been misinterpreted.

There is little doubt that the popular version of undermining and scuppering will pass into educational folklore. The *Observer* article that sparked off the controversy appeared on 22 August 1971. The Bryant and Trabasso article had appeared on 13 August 1971, but in *Nature*, a journal not usually read by those interested in discussing education. However, the controversy over educational practice is not about Piaget's work but derivations made from it by others. Piaget is being bashed for laws and practices which were not his but the work of his adaptors.

Piaget's first book was published in French in 1923. At least thirteen more books have followed, accompanied by many articles. The gaps between original and translation have stretched to seventeen years. Seven were written and translated between 1932 and 1950. There was little but academic interest in the English-speaking world until the 1950s. Then Piaget became the fashion and his influence on the Plowden Report on English primary schooling was apparent, not only in the passages on child development, but on the recommendations about curriculum and teaching methods.[9]

However, the influence was not direct, but through interpretations. Here there is a two-level growth industry. First there are texts for students of psychology. Below these are many "Piaget for teachers" books written in a simple style and justified not only because the original is difficult to read, even in translation, but because the standard psychology texts are also too tough for teachers. The sequence is translation, interpretation and simplification. Educational practice is based on these simplifications, but as Piaget was not particularly concerned with classroom practices, each simplification is also an extension of the original to cover new ground. To report that Piaget's Law has been scuppered is to attack the man for something he never formulated and to puncture a law that has never existed, by reference to a phoned account of an experiment that is itself reported in a guarded and modest style. The tragedy is that the "Piaget was wrong" headline is likely to be remembered while the article on which it is wrongly based will be read by few and will take years to appear, even in a summarised form, in an accessible educational journal or book.

Sampling

The object of research is usually to generalise about the human condition. Information has to be collected from studies of specific groups which are available and, if possible, representative. Sampling has become the systematic way of choosing a group that is small enough for convenient data collection and large enough to be representative of the population from which it has been selected.

It may, however, be difficult to define the population to be studied. Old people or adolescents are not contained in single lists and arbitrary selection has to be made from incomplete sources such as cooperative general practitioners. Criminals are sampled from prison or court records. But in these and other cases there is no exact definition of the population from which a sample can be drawn. If you do not know in advance who are included as "men in the street", it is questionable whether you can ever sample them in a representative way.

At worst a writer's views may be serving as a one-man sample. In other cases convenience or availability may have determined the sample. Unless the method of sampling is spelled out, scepticism is advisable. Students from one university department of psychology are unlikely to represent all students, all young persons or the human race. Monkeys caged in a zoo are unlikely to provide pertinent evidence for the explanation of normal human behaviour. Asylums, concentration camps and factories are often used to generalise about the organisation of schools, but it is worth remembering the differences between model and reality. However reliable the methods used in sampling, the group selected may only be representative of the specific population from which it was chosen.

This need to consider the representativeness of samples applies in all subjects. The historian has to be wary of generalising about a past population from evidence left by the rich who could afford to build to last and could leave written records. Anthropologists often observed the unusual rather than the normal and by the time observational techniques had improved, most of the small-scale societies had been colonised or fought over in the second world war. The criminologist relied on criminals who had been caught rather than those successful in getting away with crime. In all subjects the most certain way of ensuring that a work is published is to concentrate on the problems and the deviations. This is legitimate provided these are not taken as a sample of the whole population.

There are two forms of sample used in the social sciences. The judgment, purposive or quota samples are all variations on the method of selecting individuals or groups who are seen to be representative of the target population. The judgment is that of the researcher, choosing what seems to him typical, relevant or interesting. It is purposive because the choice serves the objectives of the investigation. The quota sample allows the actual collector of information to use discretion in the final choice. The probability sample by contrast is selected as far as possible to eliminate the judgment or bias of the investigator. These are sometimes called random samples because at its most refined each member of the population is given an equal chance of selection. However, lucky dips are seldom used. It is more common to take a systematic sample from a list of names. Electoral registers, doctors' lists and record cards can be used to draw every nth name according to the total size of sample required.

Random samples do not guarantee representativeness. It is bad, but random luck, to draw a sample of all millionaires in a study of income distribution. It is small consolation that from a random sample the chances of this producing the results found can be calculated. Large samples reduce this kind of mischance, but are expensive. Only the Census draws a hundred per cent or a ten per cent sample of the whole population.

The more usual procedure to ensure representation without excessive size is through stratification. This consists of breaking the population down into smaller homogeneous groups before sampling. A box of a hundred marbles, ten of ten different colours, could be sampled adequately by choosing one from each of the ten colours after they had been separated. To sample them and ensure representation without this stratification would take a much larger sample than ten. Stratification reduces the chance of fluke samples and enables the proportions in each strata to be fixed in advance. Hence most random samples ensure not an even chance of selection, but a known chance.

Judgment and probability samples are often combined. Thus a school or a factory may be selected first because it is convenient for the researcher. Then a random sample is taken within. For the reader this combination is important. The initial choice may have introduced bias which can be concealed under the mathematical calculations based on the second, random sampling. The examples that follow have been chosen because the methods of sampling are discussed by the authors. The reader is given a fair chance. They are amongst the most reliable. The most suspicious are those accounts which contain no description of sampling method. Here the third key question should be used, for the original sample determines the extent to which generalisations can be made.

PROBABILITY SAMPLING

An accessible, typical and fully described probability sample can be found in the enquiry into young school leavers carried out by the Government Social Survey for the Schools Council.[1] Here teachers, parents, thirteen to sixteen year-olds and nineteen and twenty year-olds were interviewed to get information useful for planning the raising of the school leaving age. This was a multi-stage sample, consisting of a first stage when 150 schools were sampled and then another stage when pupils, teachers and parents attached to these schools were selected.

The chances of the school being selected was determined by the number of school leavers in it. As 58 per cent of school leavers were in modern schools, 87 such schools were selected (58 per cent of 150). This method of allocating schools was continued for grammar and comprehensive schools. Then schools within each region were selected on the basis of the numbers in this age group within them. Thus 6.2 per cent of school leavers were in Wales so 5 of the 87 modern schools were picked from Wales (6.2 per cent of 87) and so on. Schools were then weighted according to the numbers of school leavers they contained and a random sample drawn from each region.

The second stage was to sample pupils and ex-pupils within the selected schools. This was done systematically from school registers, reducing the chance of bias by giving each school a random number at which to start the selection of names. In the end, 99 per cent of teachers, 94 per cent of parents, 96 per cent of thirteen to sixteen-year-olds and 71 per cent of nineteen and twenty-year-olds were interviewed. This is a base line against which other probability samples can be gauged. But the care taken was expensive, the spread of schools wide and the interviewing programme extensive. Few studies can afford to be so thorough.

PURPOSIVE SAMPLING

Goldthorpe et al, in their study of the affluent worker, had no lists available from which a probability sample could be taken.[2] To work within a budget they chose Luton as a likely town because of its prosperity, rapid growth, isolation from other traditional industrial areas, high proportion living on private housing estates and firms known for their high wages, advanced personnel and welfare services and good records of industrial relations.

This is typical of the better design of purposive sample. It focuses on a particular type of worker and a particular industrial

53

situation. Working within a small budget it was impossible to spread the interviews to other areas or to sample all workers in a particular and high income group even if this was a practical possibility. In the event, Vauxhall Motors, Skefko Ball Bearing and Laporte Chemicals were selected within Luton. These employed 30 per cent of the town's labour force. Within these firms male employees between twenty-one and forty-six, married and living with their wives, resident in Luton, earning over £17 per week gross (in October 1962) and doing jobs central to the main production systems were to be the centre of the investigation. Within each firm, therefore, certain types of worker were selected by concentrating on a limited number of departments. This was necessary because it was time-consuming to get to know how each department worked, to get the management to agree to let more than a few departments be investigated, and to get the managers, supervisors and union officials in each department to agree to the interviewing programme. Within each department the aim was to interview all men who came within the interests of the study. Only in two of the larger departments within Vauxhall Motors was a sampling of individuals necessary. This was done at random from personnel records and was the only actual random sampling. This is not therefore a random sample, but the authors argue that it is nevertheless representative of the more affluent worker. The final sample of 326 individuals was selected to investigate a hypothesis, not as a descriptive survey. Representativeness was not the primary concern of the authors and they are careful not to generalise from it to the total population of affluent workers.

Purposive sampling is very common in the social sciences and education. It is necessary to get as much information as possible about the reasons for the choice of institution or group and for any peculiarities about them. It is good practice to ask why Floud, Halsey and Martin chose South-west Hertfordshire and Middlesborough for their important study of the relation between social class and educational opportunity.[3] Similarly the question should be asked of Jackson and Marsden's study of a Huddersfield grammar school,[4] Hargreaves of Lumley Secondary Modern,[5] Wakeford on public schools,[6] and the choice of areas like Bethnal Green or Woodford[7] for community studies. In some cases it is convenience that determined choice. Thus the author made a seven-year follow up study of a college of education in which he worked because this was convenient.[8] But this has dangers, for it was an arbitrary choice and meant that complete objectivity was difficult. Again, while each article on this particular work was carefully concluded by pointing out that generalisation was impossible because of the unique character of this college, this was rapidly forgotten as the evidence was used by later writers to illustrate general points about the training of teachers. Similarly Wakeford studied the public school where he went as a pupil, had a brother attending, was a member of the old boys' association and to which he returned as a temporary assistant master to act as participant observer to collect the information for the book.[9]

Thus a look at the way the sample was chosen should be followed by a continuing lookout for generalisation from limited cases. Affluent workers, juvenile thieves, working wives, new methods of teaching children to read are studied for their topical importance. But a sample chosen for convenience, because access is easy or because the school or area has some unique characteristic limits the study as a basis for generalisation. Psychologists often use students, especially psychology students, and generalise the results to the population as a whole. Delinquents are chosen from court records or penal institutions and used to reflect on all criminals, where they may be only representative of those that get caught. Schools where the headmaster is keen to let a researcher in are not typical, while those who are buzzing with innovations are exceptional and often welcoming. Patients of psychoanalysts, pupils at progressive schools, at small experimental schools like Malting House under a teacher of Susan Isaacs' ability,[10] schools carrying out new work that attracts ambitious staff and resources from curriculum development projects, can be very misleading bases for describing the general situation. Even worse, many are prepared to discuss human behaviour on the basis of observations of rats, monkeys and other animals. Even where these observations are in the natural habitat and not by the researcher on caged animals under experimental conditions, scepticism is the safest attitude. Random samples of a population may or may not be representative. But at least this depends on chance. Where the sampling is purposive there is not even a guarantee of an even chance unless the author takes the trouble to discuss his reasons for assuming his sample is representative.

The term 'quota sampling' is often applied to the type of sampling used in market research and opinion polling. In quota sampling, the interviewer is given a list with the types of person to contact. These are usually defined by such criteria as social class, age and sex. The interviewer gets a list with the numbers she is to contact of each type. She goes, for example, to areas where the twelve working-class married women workers between twenty and thirty years old that make up one quota are liable to be found. Then there is a search for a specified number with these characteristics previously defined in the office. In practice quota sampling gives reliable results with experienced interviewers, but because it is not random, is not open to mathematical procedures that can give a level of confidence in the results obtained. The speed, cheapness and absence of problems of finding particular individuals make quota sampling useful, but it lacks the mathematical basis that can indicate the chances of the results from a random sample being due to the particular sample that has been used.

Quota sampling depends on the judgment of the investigator. The interviewer tempted to fill her quotas with the alert woman with one child rather than tackling a harried mother of four, although the latter really fits the quota definition, is in the same position as the research worker tempted to use school X instead of Y because the former is welcoming and convenient. In both personal bias is entering before information has been collected and the outcome may be tinged by this subjective element.

In some cases quota sampling has to be used because it is impossible to find lists from which a probability sample of a population can be drawn. Thus there is no way of listing affluent workers or children of very high ability. They can only be sampled by choosing likely firms or schools and contacting those that fall within the definition of this particular population. The alternative is to take a very large probability sample and analyse separately those that fall into the appropriate categories.

One particularly hazardous form of purposive sampling is the use of volunteers. Regardless of the safeguards that are built in, the reader is right to suspect that there is something unusual about those who step forward when a researcher asks for help. The most famous example of this is the Kinsey Report on human sexual behaviour.[11] Kinsey was determined to get a large sample and organised a campaign to interest clubs, families and other groups to volunteer. His object was to get 100 per cent samples from a number of different groups. However, while his final sample numbered 12,000, a minority were completed groups. Kinsey was aware of the dangers of volunteers and built in cross checking techniques to detect distortions. This was a reason for wanting complete families or groups, for the answers could then be checked against others in the group.

The first volunteers were found to include many who were active, aggressive and exhibitionist. Kinsey tried therefore to obtain more reluctant volunteers by his recruiting campaign. He appealed for volunteers in the name of science, tried to establish advanced rapport in communities and to establish a reputation for scrupulous anonymity. But the suspicion remains that in such an intimate enquiry, those who come forward for interview are also those who are advanced in their behaviour. Furthermore, some groups such as homosexuals may be very reluctant to volunteer for fear of blackmail or prosecution, however secure the information was actually kept.

Dependence on volunteers is rare, but often someone in authority or position of influence may provide the volunteers. Thus Veness, in her study of school leavers, first got permission from the education officers of a county and then invited headteachers to volunteer their schools for investigation.[12] Similarly Phillips got information on small social groups in England from friends willing to help.[13] Work relying on such samples must be read as illustrations of the attitudes and behaviour of those who are cooperative or are not in a position to say no. Similarly, samples from those attending clubs, those at home during the day or using public libraries are not likely to be typical. A study such as Hemming's *Problems of Adolescent Girls*, based on 3,259 letters to a weekly journal between April 1953 and March 1955, is representative only of girls who write about their problems to magazine aunties.[14] The greatest blunder in survey history was the 1936 Literary Digest poll, predicting that Landon would defeat Roosevelt, on the basis of a postal questionnaire from a sample drawn from the telephone directory, thus eliminating many poorer voters.[15]

There is no simple way of assessing whether a sample is adequate. Three important features of sampling have to be considered. First, as long as sampling is being used it is a matter of how much chance there is of freak samples being drawn, never a matter of certainty. This is why results from random sampling are expressed in terms of probability or levels of confidence. Secondly, the larger the sample, the more confidence there can be that a freak selection will not be made. Thirdly, the greater the variety of the characteristics in the population being measured the larger the sample needs to be.

The last point has already been discussed. One tin soldier from thousands from the same run of production suffices as a test of quality because they are all similar. But the physical features of humans and even more their behaviour and attitudes are very varied and a larger sample is needed. The greater the spread of the feature being measured around the mean, the larger the sample size has to be. This is why stratification is commonly used, for it arranges the population into groups so that each contains persons of similar age, class, education and so on, thus reducing the necessary sample size.

The confidence that can be placed in the adequacy of a sample therefore varies inversely with the distribution of the characteristics being measured and directly with the numbers in the sample.

RESPONSE

The care with which a sample has been designed will be wasted if those chosen cannot be found or refuse to cooperate. The response rate is probably the most important single indicator of the reliability of a survey. The reader should try to find evidence that response has been considered as a design problem, that there were efforts to minimise non-response and that there was some attempt to investigate the character of the non-responders. Finally, the frankness with which the author discusses the response issue can be taken as an index of his concern to give the reader the chance to assess the dependability of the work.

The following are samples of response rates in different types of survey.

Postal questionnaires

R.R. DALE, *Mixed or Single-sex School*?[16] Colleges sent questionnaires, response rate, 42 per cent.

J. GABRIEL, *The Emotional Problems of the Teacher in the Classroom*,[17] response rate to first questionnaire to individual teachers, 35 per cent, second questionnaire, 29 per cent.

F. MUSGROVE, *Youth and the Social Order*.[18] Questionnaire to adults in towns, response rate, 32 per cent, in suburbs, 34 per cent.

Surveys using interviews

J. and E. NEWSON, *Infant Care in an Urban Community*.[19] Response rate 92 per cent, including 1.6 per cent refusals.

P. WILLMOTT, *Adolescent Boys of East London*,[20] Response rate 88 per cent, including 8 per cent refusals.

D. GLASS, ed. *Social Mobility*,[21] study based on interviews by the Social Survey, initial response rate 77.5%, 3.4% refusals. Substitutes used to raise final response rate to 93%.

Follow up studies

M.L. KELLMER PRINGLE, N.R. BUTLER *and* R. DAVIE, *11,000 Seven-Year-Olds*.[22] Of the 17,000 babies born 3 to 9 March 1958,

15,300 could be traced in 1964. Information was collected on 11,000 of these by mid 1965.

J.W.B. DOUGLAS, *The Home and School*,[23] contained full information from 3,418 from sample first drawn in 1946. In 1948, 4,742 completed interviews and in 1950, 4,668. During the first four years of the children's lives, 4.3 per cent died and 4.5 per cent emigrated. By the time of the Home and School survey, 4.9 per cent had died and 6.7 per cent had emigrated.

F.W. MILLER and others, *Growing up in Newcastle upon Tyne*,[24] studied 847 five-year-olds out of the 1,142 children born between 1 May and 30 June 1947; 49 had died, 239 moved away and 7 left the survey by 1952.

These figures bring out important points about the design of surveys. First, postal questionnaries usually get very low response. Secondly, well organised interview programmes can obtain around a 90 per cent response. The Government Social Survey usually attain this figure. Third, follow-up studies suffer from great difficulties in tracing the original sample.

The importance of looking carefully at the proportion not responding lies in the possibility that they are not a random sample and may not be similar to those who respond. The interview technique has the advantage that the refusals can be assessed. But in the postal questionnaire, there is no way of knowing whether those who did not reply forgot, were too scared to answer or rugged individualists who would have liked to have told the sender to get lost. There is always the suspicion that the non-responders may have been the most interesting and certainly the most non-conformist group. Thus an attempt in the Authoritarian Personality study to use mailed questionnaires was abandoned, not only because only 20 per cent responded, but because those that did reply were found to be biased in a democratic direction.[25]

Non-response also makes it difficult to interpret generalisations. If 100 out of 200 respond and 90 of these answer YES, does this mean that 90 per cent are in favour or 45 per cent? There is no way of really knowing, although the assumption is usually that those who replied are representative and a huge majority are in favour. But the half who did not reply may have been so violently opposed that they tore up the questionnaire and threw it in the fire.

It is therefore important to look for attempts to anticipate and reduce non-response. Calling back on those who were not in when the interviewer called usually finds a few more. The Government Social Survey insists that it is the duty of an interviewer to call at any time, however inconvenient, or to fix an appointment for a later period to get near a complete response. Even where refusal or failure to contact is finally accepted, there should have been some attempt to assess the characteristics of non-responders. Similarly a follow-up letter with another stamped addressed envelope can bring in more completed forms from a postal questionnaire.

These additions to those responding are not only important in themselves, but can be used to see whether those who cannot be contacted at first or do not reply differ in any systematic way from those responding at first. This is the only way of estimating whether non-responders differ from responders. Thus if it is found that half the people who cannot be contacted in a survey are young married couples, this proportion can be used if it has been decided to bring the number up to that originally intended by additions after failure to contact.

Finally, it must be remembered that non-response occurs only in probability sampling. In purposive samples contacts are made until a quota is filled. The advantages of probability samples are in providing a reliable basis for generalisation and for mathematical calculations. But very often non-response makes a mockery of any complex statistical calculations. It is the way statistics can lend an aura of competence to inadequate samples that makes it essential to find response rates. Studies have been discussed here because they contained these rates. None are therefore as suspect as those in which non-response rates have been omitted.

All research depends on observation. Through the ears and eyes the material and social world is interpreted. But this perception is not passive. Impressions are first selected and then interpreted within the mind of the observer. Between the impression on the senses and the reported interpretation are the attitudes, values and prejudices, as well as the academic conceptual models, of the researcher. Perception is the process of fitting what is seen or heard into these maps and frameworks in the mind.

A psychologist may see a classroom as a situation of organised learning experiences reinforcing correct and inhibiting incorrect answers. A sociologist may see the same scene as a group constrained by the power of the teachers and the interaction of peers. A teacher may see it as a situation to be controlled, a parent as a group affecting their child, a head teacher as a reflection on the competence of the teacher and an inspector as a guide to the efficiency of the school. Individuals enter situations with maps already established in their minds into which they fit the evidence of their senses.

The effect of cultural differences on observation can be gauged from the improbable but delightful contrast between German and American psychologists observing hungry rats confronted by a maze in which food was available at the far end. Both sets of rats learned to traverse the maze. But those seen by the Germans sat pondering the problem in an immobile way until a solution dawned and they threaded their way through. American rats, however, launched themselves hell for leather in a series of bruising trial runs until they learned from their errors. The time taken was similar, the style contrasting. Any student who has puzzled over the differences between gestalt and behaviourist theories of learning will realise that this ludicrous picture reflects an underlying discrepancy due to national differences which seem to have established different frames of reference in the minds of the two national groups which developed these theories.

A more serious if still amusing example of the effects of the expectations of the observer can be demonstrated by Rosenthal and Fode's experiment with twelve psychology students asked to measure the time taken for rats to learn to run to the darker arm of a maze to find food.[1] Sixty ordinary rats were divided between the students, but six students were told they had maze-bright rats and six were given maze-dull rats, each sample said to be specially bred. Each rat was given ten chances each day for five days to learn that the darker arm led to food.

While there was no actual difference in the maze-learning ability of the rats, the students observed the results that they were led to anticipate by the description of their sample as bright or dull. The bright rats not only became better performers but showed daily improvement, while the dull rats only improved to the third day and then deteriorated. Furthermore, the dull rats refused to start at all more frequently than the eager-to-get-with-it bright ones and were slower to reach the end after they had learned. After the experiment was over the students rated their rats and their own attitudes towards them. Those having "bright" rats viewed them as brighter, more pleasant and more likeable, and their own attitude towards the rats was more relaxed and enthusiastic than among the six students with the "dull" sample.

Such effects are not confined to the social sciences, although the frequent use of human beings as subjects of research makes them more prone to self-fulfilling effects. In the natural sciences a researcher can be similarly misled, either by the expectations of colleagues or his own predictions and hopes. Once set to expect a result, a scientist in all fields is liable to find his observations biased. This is why controls and repetitions of experiments by others are so important. In the natural sciences the use of measuring instruments eliminates much of the dependence on human perception, but bias still occurs. This is the central paradox of science.

In 1903 Blondlot announced the discovery of n-rays, which gave no photographic effect but could be detected through observing their effect on the luminosity of phosphorescent surfaces. The discovery was quickly confirmed by other French scientists and by 1904, seventy-seven scientific publications had included descriptions of the applications of these rays, how to detect them, the materials that emitted them, their wavelength and spectrum. Yet outside France no one seemed to be able to detect n-rays through replicating Blondlot's work. In 1904, shortly after Blondlot had been awarded the Lalande prize for his discovery, the rays were shown to be the result of his faulty observations. The discovery of X-rays by Rontgen in 1896 had led to a great interest in such phenomena, and Blondlot and others were too ready to be convinced by their own fallible perception. After 1909 the n-ray passed out of science, its discoverer having gone mad. Poor Professor Rene or Prosper or plain M. Blondlot, Blondot or Blandot: even in death he is not respected, for these three versions of his name appeared in the three references cited here.[2]

This long introduction has been necessary, not only because information is collected through observation alone, but because observation is a part of every research technique. Humans involved in investigating have to try to control the factors that could bias their own perceptions. This is not easy, for most of these influences have been learned and are tied up with personal hopes, fears, ambitions and needs. The investigator is always a factor in the experimental situation.

Once again the social scientist faces a unique difficulty. Most observation is also interaction. The researcher is also being observed. His presence will disturb the natural scene. The behaviour he sees may be a response to his presence.

THE CONTROL OF OBSERVATION

In the history of science it is often difficult to sort out fiction from genuine scientific theory. Science has always been mixed up with religion and mysticism. Astrology and alchemy contained astronomy and chemistry. Men practised 'mysteries', sought the Philosopher's Stone, elixirs and magic numbers. As they did so scientific techniques were developed. A man like Leonardo da Vinci was artist, visionary and scientist. Teilhard de Chardin in the twentieth century similarly mixed imagination with scientific fact. Science has drawn inspiration from the artist and the scientist has inspired the artist.

The social sciences are similarly rooted in traditions where imagination and observation are fused. Many books are based on imagination or casual memories. Others draw on the memories of others and trust that the questions asked got valid replies. Others are just the opinions of the author. Yet all may be classified as social science and be written in the customary, convincing style. Libraries are graveyards testifying to the fallibility of armchair theorising of this kind. Books remain on shelves to confuse the living.

The pollution of interpretation with personal interests, values and memories makes it important to look for controls over reported observations. Again, it is the casual observation or those studies where no actual techniques are reported that are suspect. Only those studies careful enough to give the reader sufficient information can be criticised.

The first set of controls exists within subject disciplines. An anthropologist in a tribal community, a psychologist peering at children through a one-way mirror or a sociologist lurking round a crowd at a football match are, in part at least, controlled by the discipline they practise and have learned. The observations are fitted into specific subject frameworks and there converted into anthropological, psychological or sociological facts, open to criticism by colleagues.

Studies can also be controlled through preliminary fixing of the conditions under which observation is to be made. This can consist of controls over what is to be looked at, how and when it is to be viewed or how the information is to be recorded. The aim is to build in checks over the observer and to enable those that read or follow him to know exactly what was observed, to replicate and check the results. Teams of observers, timed observations, check lists, films and tape recordings have all been used to eliminate dependence on the unaided individual.

Reiss has argued that there is no necessary distinction between observational techniques and social surveying either in power to discover the new or in control over the research process.[3] He used carefully selected, trained and supervised observers to study crime and the work of the police in metropolitan areas. There were standardised procedures for recording events as they happened. The thirty-six observers, selected from over two hundred who were interviewed for the job, were allocated to eight areas with high crime rates in each of three cities. In each city, days, police watches and beats were sampled. Every effort was made to detect and reduce errors in observing by regular supervision.

THE DEGREE OF DETACHMENT

Observers can either participate in the activity they are observing, remain detached or, as is most usual, adopt some position in between. Only in those rare cases where one-way mirrors or some other screening device are used, or the observed are oblivious to the presence of an observer, are the subtle adjustments due to social interaction missing. These adjustments effect the behaviour of both observer and observed.

The decision over the degree of involvement in the activity to be observed is usually made after considering the possible distorting effect on the activity through the presence of an observer. A fully participant observer may fit in with the group so smoothly that it will go on behaving naturally. This is particularly the case where members of the group do not know that one or more of their number are observers gathering information. But even where the researcher is known to be after information, he may be accepted and little distortion may result.

Participant observation is valuable because it enables groups to be observed in an unforced situation. Its weakness comes from the same situation. The act of becoming involved threatens the maintenance of objectivity. Thus the reader should still be asking the basic questions, how reliable is this observation, how valid are the results? The results of participant observation may be valid because there has been no distortion of the situation, but reliability is doubtful. Another observer might see things very differently once he started to participate and observe.

This is, once again, the fundamental dilemma of social science. Involvement is necessary for understanding, but science is a detached activity. An American watching his first cricket match could soon explain the action by referring it to his previous experience. But only by getting among cricketers and preferably playing the game could he come to understand it and interpret it accurately. But this involvement would lead to affection, emotion replacing detached assessment. Western observers of simple societies face the same difficulty. So do observers of children, youth groups, gangs, dropouts and drug addicts.

Frankenberg sees participant observation as proceeding through an early stage of acclimatisation within the culture being studied, to an internalisation of that culture.[4] From this point the observer has learned a new perspective that he can draw on in addition to his own native view of the world. But a final stage has to be reached in order to communicate with an audience. At this point the involvement gives way again to objectivity. This sequence occurs in all social scientific research and illustrates the dilemma of balancing involvement and detachment. Stage one is liable to involve harsh judgements on the group being studied. Stage two is liable to involve a romantic, tolerant view and stage three will be marked by a return to objective, yet informed attitudes.

THE EFFECT OF PARTICIPATING ON THE OBSERVER

The reflections of participant observers have dramatically illustrated the impact of involvement on the observer. Thus Gans, studying the American middle class in Leavittown tried to remain the outsider but was subject to an internal tug-of-war as the community involved him.[5] The difficulty of gaining entry and acceptance, the urge to have someone to talk to about the work and the feeling that he was inevitably deceiving people increased the strain.

Gans has also suggested that field work attracts those who are in some way alienated from their own background. Participating and observing becomes therefore an educating process. This is illustrated in the three central essays of Vidich, Bensman, and Stein's collection, *Reflections on Community Studies*.[6] Seeley, discussing his work in Crestwood Heights, contrasts theorising about society with actually entering a society.[7] The sociology he was taught seemed disembodied, a sophisticated, shared illusion. This innocence was shattered when he got into the field. The neat theory was disintegrated by the reality. But the research also forced him to analyse the relation between his own childhood experience, his personality and his choice of profession.

Stein reflecting on his own prior analysis of community studies also detected a personal conviction, based on his experiences in the field, that the sociology he had learned and the techniques for collecting information that were recommended could not generate insight.[8] To participate and understand in a concrete situation meant first detaching oneself from the standards of professional sociology.

Wolff, who spent periods spread over twenty years studying a community in New Mexico, uses the word surrender to describe his experience.[9] He became totally involved and shelved theoretical ideas as he immersed himself in the community. Wolff, like Stein and Seeley, found the human situation too complex, too emotional, to match the neutral systems of sociological theory. All these writers had also to work out fresh methods of research suitable for a situation in which they were deeply involved and in which accepted methodology with its emphasis on objectivity was inadequate.

At the other extreme from the attempt to get accepted within the group to be studied is non-participant observation, in which the observer remains deliberately detached. This not only eliminates the chance of his perception of the situation being biased by his affection for the group and eliminates the chance of members feeding him with false information, but enables the maximum number of controls to be established over the observation. But there is an accompanying risk that lack of insight will result from lack of involvement. The meaning of events may be misunderstood.

The examples that follow have been chosen to illustrate participant and non-participant observation. They are also ranged from the tightly controlled observations of Bales to the more usual methods of Whyte, where there was little attempt to enforce predetermined methods of observation.

THE ETHICS OF OBSERVATION

In all observational studies there is an issue of confidence The researcher is asking for co-operation or observing without explaining the situation to those observed. In the first case, the ethical question arises over what to publish, for those who have agreed to participate may object to published accounts of their behaviour. In the second case the observer is a voyeur and his report may have all the intimacy of a Peeping Tom's notebook and all its legitimacy.

This issue is complicated by the dilemma that the scientist is in if he starts observing without the consent of the observed or by clandestine means. He is nevertheless a scientist committed to report what he finds and not to conceal information or distort it to protect his informants. This dilemma can be followed in the work of Whyte on street corner gangs.[10] Here it was a combination of respect for those who had befriended him and provided the information, coupled with a fear that adverse accounts of them would put the author in danger of being carved up. Whyte's study lasted four years. By the end he was playing an active part in Cornerville society. To his informants he was writing a book. He visited them after publication to gauge its impact. Perhaps this is an indication of the compromise nature of the book. Nevertheless it remains a classic, and its methodological appendix has a full discussion of the ethical issues.

A similar case was the study of a small town by Bensman and Vidich.[11] Here the presence of the social scientists was not realised by the inhabitants. Vidich has discussed the dilemma of publication, but in this case the decision was to publish because scientific procedures took precedence over obligations to the town. The difficulty here is that all fictionally named towns, schools and organisations are soon known by name. To Bensman and Vidich this was a refusal to fix the data to avoid exposing the private lives of the citizens. It could be argued, however, that the original decision to gather information surreptitiously was itself unethical.

Probably the most fascinating but most morally dubious study was Festinger, Riecken and Schachter's *When Prophecy Fails*.[12] Here the authors and their students infiltrated a group who had prophesied that the end of the world was nigh. The social scientists were fully accepted and even after the world carried on passed its predicted end, another observer was introduced to check on the impact of this miscalculation on the group. Recording was done in the toilet, out on the porch or on midget tape recorders. This was an extreme example, but most social scientists have experienced moments when they have access to information that is obviously private. Publish and be damned can be justified on scientific grounds, but a public conned once is unlikely to co-operate again. Furthermore, social scientists are not exempt from the responsibility to exercise power over others with restraint.

THE LIMITS ON OBSERVATION AS A TECHNIQUE

The four dilemmas just outlined indicate the perfect design for an observational study. It would be fully controlled to ensure reliability. It would be fully participant to ensure maximum insight. It would be carried out and reported with scientific rigour. It would be done from planning to publication with the full knowledge of the observed. Inevitably, however, these four conditions work against one another. Full control and full participation are usually incompatible. Scientific rigour will usually disturb the rapport of observed and observer and is a difficult role to maintain while participating. Once the observed realise they are being studied their behaviour is liable to become unnatural and they are very likely to object to some intimate detail being published.

Here again is the recurring problem of the clash of reliability and validity. At one extreme are the studies of Bales.[13] Small groups, in specially designed rooms being observed and recorded by specially trained observers sitting behind one-way mirrors, were profiled for the interaction that occurred between them as they solved problems. Here the observers were checked against each other, against expert recorders and against their own previous performance, until they had attained a high level of reliability. But the obvious criticism is that the situation was so artificial that the results have no significance for normal conditions. This is the direct contrast to Whyte's study of gangs where insight was given priority over reliability.

Most observational studies lie between these extremes and suffer some diminution of both validity and reliability. Thus Hargreaves's study of a secondary modern school is typical of those educational studies that lie between extremes aiming at insight or reliability.[14] Here a combination of testing and observation was used. The problems that arose are fully discussed. The teachers knew what was happening and Hargreaves taught part time while researching for the remainder. The difficulties arose out of the casual remarks by staff that were significant, placing him in the moral dilemma already discussed. The staff also saw him as a useful source of information on boys and on other teachers, and his name was used to try to influence events. Finally he had to give up teaching lower stream boys in order to get valid information from them. Observation in schools, in factories and anywhere containing formal differences in rank is complicated by the suspicion of one group if rapport is established with another.

The Hargreaves study has been only one of many case studies of single schools. These have usually started as higher degree theses.

All raise problems of the confidence between researcher and subject organisation, especially centred on what should be published. Social scientists are trained to be detached observers, for accurate observation is at the heart of scientific activity. But detachment can obscure the subtler details of human activity and increase the chance of the observer imposing his own scientific straitjacket on his subjects and reducing them to puppets. Because observation is at the heart of things it is most vulnerable to the confusion of everyday and scientific definitions of the situation.

Controversy 3
Do the public want religious education in state schools?

This controversy revolves around a simple question about the attitude of the public towards religious education in schools. That each party in the dispute can present evidence to support its own case is explicable in the light of the preceding chapters. But here another feature is significant. Two of the surveys involved were carried out by the same research agency. Yet the results still reflected the opposed views of the two bodies paying for the survey.

Every state school in England must hold a daily act of worship and give lessons in religious instruction. The controversy over these clauses in the Education Act of 1944 has been continuous in the history of state schooling. Outraged humanists battle with entrenched churchmen. In the middle the public seems to become increasingly apathetic. Given the confusing nature of the evidence the antagonists provide, this public apathy is fair criticism of what is claimed to be conclusive evidence.

Here two surveys supporting extreme views will be compared. Both were based on probability samples of around 2,000 persons. Both used interviewers asking apparently simple questions. Both were carried out by National Opinion Polls.

The survey commissioned by *New Society* and reported by Goldman in 1965 claimed that 90 per cent of the sample wanted the present arrangements to continue and for religious instruction in schools to remain unchanged in both primary and secondary schools.[1] The survey commissioned in 1969 by the British Humanist Association found that out of eight objectives of schooling, the sample ranked "help in becoming a convinced

73

Christian" and "information about Christianity and other world religions" sixth and seventh for boys and sixth and fifth for girls over twelve years old.[2] The conclusion drawn here was that there was no real expression of support for the retention of religious instruction. Barring some dramatic change in public attitude in four years, the neutral conclusion is that in some no doubt honest way, the opinions of the sponsors had percolated into the research design.

The questions themselves give no obvious clue to the way this bias could have been introduced. The descriptions of the research are inadequate for any other part of the design to be examined thoroughly.

The *New Society* survey asked "Should the present school religious arrangements continue"? and "Do you want religious instruction as it is, or none"? Ninety per cent replied "yes" and "as it is". The Humanist Association claimed that this was the equivalent of asking "Do you like tea?" and taking the answer "yes" to mean a dislike of coffee, as no alternative form of moral education was offered. Curiously, they chose the same research agency to do their own survey.

The 1969 British Humanist Association survey used show cards on which the key question was "which of the following do you think is most important in the education of schoolboys (schoolgirls) over the age of twelve years?" There followed a list of objectives in schooling. Only 4 per cent chose "information about Christianity and other world religions" or "help in becoming a convinced Christian" for boys and 5 per cent for girls. Given the obvious importance of the other objectives it could be argued that these questions were the equivalent of asking people to chose whether water or tea was more important for survival.

If extreme views seem to produce extreme answers to questions, do agencies having no strong views get compromise answers? The 1966 Schools Council Enquiry Number 1 (*Young School Leavers*) seems to suggest that they do.[3] This survey was only concerned to rank groups of subjects. The Government Social Survey asked, "Do you think it is very important, fairly important or not important that (name of parent's child) should be taught (subjects) at school?" There were thirteen groups of subjects. Religious instruction was seen as very important for boys by 43 per cent of the sample and for girls by 45 per cent. For boys and girls alike religious instruction was ranked seventh out of the thirteen groups in the percentage seeing it as very important.

This conflicting evidence could only aggravate the existing confusion over the religious issue in English education. Not surprisingly the 1970 Durham Report on religious education referred to actual surveys of opinion on only one of its 577 pages and then only to gauge whether England was or was not a Christian country.[4] The efforts to survey public opinion were either ignored, not considered valuable or not known to the authors.

Information through asking questions

If you want an answer, ask a question. Whether it is an attempt to reconstruct the past, describe the present or predict the future, the questionnaire and the interview have come to dominate the collection of information in the social sciences, particularly sociology. Yet, "When did you last . . . ?", "How many times did you . . . ?" and "How will you . . . ?" are questions that will not just produce answers but will reconstruct the meaning of the situation in which the asker and answerer are involved. The asking of questions is the main source of social scientific information about everyday behaviour, yet between question and answer there may be shifts in the relation between scientist and subject. The final answers emerge from this interaction and the meanings that each party gives to the situation. The questions have created this situation and the answers are meaningful only in its context.

Asking questions to get valid answers is therefore a skilled and sensitive job requiring knowledge of the environment in which the questionnaire is to be filled in or the interview conducted. It requires knowledge of the likely impact of questionner on respondent. It requires a sensitivity to the symbolic sophistication of humans, non-verbal as well as verbal. Imagine, with Jowell and Hoinville, a poll conducted among coloured immigrants to discover their attitudes towards subsidised repatriation to their country of origin shortly after a speech by Enoch Powell.[1] Such a poll for Panorama by Opinion Research Centre asked such questions as "Would you like to return to your country of origin if you received financial help?" Asked this way a majority might be expected to say "yes". But now imagine the question being asked by white, middle-class, middle-aged women interviewers, on a rainy, cold day in late November in the middle of the Black Country. To anyone even capable of envisaging Trinidad or Jamaica the answers "Yes", "No" or "Don't know" are more likely to have meant "Yes please", "Get lost" or "How much!" A thought about the interaction and shifting of ground that was likely to have occurred in those macabre interviews should say more than any interactionist treatise. Yet similar scenes must have been enacted in the accumulation of the evidence on race relations in Controversy.[7]

There is a whole spectrum of situations in the use of questionnaires and interviews, ranging from the postal questionnaire where there is no direct contact to the psychoanalyst's couch where there is much. The same problems are present as in observational studies, particularly those of the degree of control and the amount of interaction. The postal questionnaire is not exempt. A parallel is the filling in of an income tax return and its interpretation by the Inland Revenue Inspector. The difficulty of the public in filling in a form designed for simplicity, the problems of the Inspector in sorting out genuine from bogus claims and the general puzzling out of how the other party responded or will respond to the questions and answers gives a good idea of the design difficulties and the interaction, even when there has been no personal contact.

There is, however, the extra factor in the interview of the two personalities involved. Interaction now is not only structured by the questions, but by personal feelings. The choice between questionnaires and interviews is usually determined by the high cost of the latter, but it is, once again, also a choice between reliability and insight. Adjustments can be made in interviews and answers can be probed. The cost is in reliability, for if the same interview was done by another interviewer the chance of identical results would usually be low. Agencies like the Government Social Survey obtain high reliability by sticking to set questions and probes, but few organisations are so scrupulous, few studies lend themselves to such rigid questions and there is always the effect of non-verbal clues intervening.

A tale by Blackburn serves to illustrate the need for caution over the validity and permanence of answers from questions.[2] A month after the publication of the influential and carefully designed study of affluent workers at Vauxhalls in Luton, maintaining that 77 per cent of workers were contented with management and working conditions, there was an open revolt with the singing of the Red Flag, a storming of the management offices and threats of lynching for the directors. The opinions expressed in answer to questions may be short-lived and shallow, but once written into articles and books, or incorporated into lectures they acquire a permanence that belies their actual instability. There are quick profits to be made from questionnaires. Productivity can be boosted by the use of computers. The consumer needs the protection of a few basic guides to quality.

WAS THERE A PILOT STUDY?

Whenever questions are to be asked and a choice made from a limited list of answers it is a safeguard if they are tried out in advance. This is a way to avoid many of the mistakes described in the rest of this chapter. The trial run checks that the questions are feasible for the sample. Pilot studies are essential for ensuring that the responses offered as possible answers actually do exhaust all the possibilities. Only by giving a free choice at this stage can all the possible answers be gauged. Some questions may be found useless as the range of answers will be limitless. Others will be found to force similar choices on everyone. Others will be beyond the understanding of the sample. Others will be greeted with derision.

Ideally the answers offered should exhaust all the possibilities and not overlap with each other. In practice respondents often find it difficult to choose an answer that fits their views. Similarly the "don't know" answer may be found to be used not only by the ignorant, but by those who can not find an answer that fits their attitudes. This type of feasibility study in advance usually combines a check on possible questions with free-ranging unstructured questions allowing the pilot sample to give their own views on the subject under study. In some cases the open-ended enquiry may form a first pilot study and the actual testing of questions a second stage. Without any pilot stage, the actual research is likely to address unsuitable questions to bewildered people.

HOW LONG WAS IT?

A skilled interviewer may be able to sustain interest and co-operation through a long session. Sessions of six to eight hours have been achieved.[3] At the other extreme, long postal questionnaires are probably never the basis of published work as not even the usual 30 per cent survive the wastepaper basket. The actual length depends on the nature of the sample and the motivation created by the topic. The span of attention of children increases only slowly with age. Old people tire easily. Head teachers, business men and the upper middle class are impatient with any form that may be time-wasting. The span of interest may increase with education but so does scepticism.

HOW DIFFICULT WERE THE QUESTIONS?

Questions can be too technical or complex. Payne reports trick questions producing support for fictitious Acts and even obtained a substantial percentage in favour of incest.[4] People are wary of admitting ignorance of an issue. The slightest clue will then be used as a guide to an answer. Some words have no precise meaning. The establishment, democracy and big business can raise emotions but obscure issues. "Fair" is not an alternative answer to "good" or "bad" as it has many meanings. The author was once alerted to a survey that indicated an alarming increase in spirit-drinking among schoolchildren. The university department concerned had found many children going to the toilets for a whisky. Fortunately this was corrected before publication as all the teachers concerned knew that this was local slang for masturbation. Once again there is the tendency for social scientists to impose their definitions on terms which have their own everyday meaning.

Even when words are straightforward, they can form a question that can baffle the public. In long questions asking for a choice between alternatives, the last is more often chosen because the first has been forgotten. A good criterion if the actual questions are available in the article or book is to check that they can be understood. The author should not be given the benefit of the doubt unless it was a survey of the sophisticated. Readers of social science are more than usually articulate and often are skilled in sorting out the obscure. The general public who are the usual respondents would flounder where the initiated are merely perplexed.

COULD THE QUESTIONS HAVE SUGGESTED THE ANSWERS?

Controversy 3 in this book is a study of attitudes towards religious education. Two surveys carried out by the same research organisation produced completely opposed results, each supporting the conflicting parties that sponsored them. It is not that leading questions are deliberately used, but that it is very difficult not to use them. This is why groups for or against legal abortion, the Common Market, capital punishment, blood sports and the Sunday opening of Welsh pubs can produce convincing evidence to support their case by taking to the streets with a questionnaire. This is rarely dishonesty. It is sometimes technical incompetence. It is often innocence of the ease with which questions can be asked to get the results that are wanted.

The following question was the basis of an article maintaining that large numbers of reluctant teachers were entering colleges of education.[5] "If you were quite free to choose, and could obtain the qualifications necessary, what field of employment would you ideally like to enter?" Fifty-three per cent of the students in colleges of education to whom this question was put indicated some profession other than teaching. Yet given the nature of the question it is remarkable that any opted for teaching. It is not known whether any other professional group would have this or any other degree of commitment for the authors did not provide this basis for comparison.

WAS PRESTIGE OR EMOTION INVOLVED?

Advertisers exploit the ease with which people can be led to associate themselves with the prestigeful. All the best people soak their teeth overnight in *X* after seducing their girl friend with gin and *Y* tonic. It may not seem decent to admit that the wogs begin at Boulogne and it is better to say you read the *Spectator* than *Playboy*. Questions can easily lead people to choose right not real answers. Furthermore, there may always be a reluctance to use the "don't know" category. None of us likes to be made to seem ignorant, especially about an issue that the man with the schedule obviously thinks important.

COULD THE ENVIRONMENT HAVE INFLUENCED THE ANSWERS?

Where questions are asked about life in schools, old people's homes, prisons or other relatively closed organisations, there may be pressure to give answers within a particular context. Again right not real answers appear. The author, comparing responses from the same students on questionnaires and interviews in a college of education had to scrap the use of unverified questionnaires because students were giving the answers they thought students in training should give.[6] Only when group discussions were held to examine the discrepancy in answers was this innocent deception uncovered. Yet combinations of methods facilitating such cross-checking are rare. Usually a single instrument is considered enough.

WHEN WERE ANSWERS CODIFIED?

Questions can be unstructured giving the respondent a free rein to answer at will, or structured, giving him only a choice of answers listed by the researcher. In the first case the researcher takes the answers and sorts them out into categories after collection. In the latter type this categorisation is done before the start of data collection. In both cases the researcher is imposing his social scientific framework around the possible common sense answers of his respondents. There is rarely a perfect fit. There is usually a pruning and bending to make the irregular everyday responses fit into the categories prepared for them. This happens in both sequences. But leaving the categorisation to the end by using open-ended, unstructured questions leaves a lot to the discretion of the researcher and this particular Procrustean bed is hidden from the reader.

The dangers of using questionnaires can best be illustrated by looking at the best research designs. The Authoritarian Personality studies have been subject to detailed analysis by Hyman and Sheatsley.[7] They acknowledge that it has hardly been rivalled for scope, prestige and influence. The work combined questionnaires and clinical interviews, the former being used to select extreme scorers on scales measuring potential Fascism for detailed analysis.

The questionnaires were first tried out on students and then adults in 1945. Hyman and Sheatsley maintain that despite the careful design the questions forced subjects to choose extreme answers without having the scope to qualify these. Yet this lack of qualification was later taken as an indication of a tendency to stereotype minority groups. By limiting the choice, the researchers produced extreme responses and then pointed out the significance of this polarisation.

The Institute of Race Relations' scale for measuring tolerance reported in Controversy[7] was criticised in a similar way for having a built-in bias towards tolerance. The difficulty here is that one man's tolerance is another's prejudice. Even more significant, Frenkel-Brunswick, one of the authors of the Authoritarian Personality, looking back at the research after a decade had passed, recognised that she and her colleagues were probably influenced by the anti-Fascist climate of opinion in the immediate post-1945 years.[8] Questions about sensitive areas of human experience are difficult to word neutrally. Even if this is accomplished the results are probably invalid within a short period as the words summing up these results will have changed.

Interviews not only depend on the quality of the questions asked, but on the awareness of, and control over, the interaction involved. The interview can be more flexible than the questionnaire, it can probe deeper, can be adjusted to circumstances, can increase rapport and co-operation. But the cost may be a reduction in control and consequently in reliability. As these issues are discussed in the following pages, it must be remembered that there is always interaction involved in the filling in of questionnaires.

The way clues can be incidentally presented and skilfully interpreted can be gauged from Pfungst's investigation of Clever Hans, a horse that could apparently solve mathematical problems, spell and identify musical notes by nodding his head, tapping his feet or pointing to letters on a board.[9] Public and experts were baffled and his master, Van Osten, a schoolmaster, made no profit from the act. Pfungst, by diligently controlling factors in the environment of the performance found that although Clever Hans could answer even when the question was not even spoken, the questioner had to be present and seen by the horse. He noticed how tense the questioner got as the horse appeared to starting to tap or point to the right answer. Pfungst now saw what all animal trainers rely on, that the horse could detect these slight involuntary clues. Pfungst even learned the trick himself so that, on all fours and blindfolded, he could answer questions from his audience without them being spoken. If a horse can detect such muscular movements as clues, man, the symbol-using animal must respond to much more than mere questions in an interview situation.

If the reader can get past the substance of the Kinsey Reports to the sections on method, they will find an acid test of interviewing.[10] It was necessary to stop any tendency to brag or distort as the sample were volunteers. Many indeed seemed to want to measure their sexual prowess against others. Complete confidentiality, absolute privacy during interviewing and no suggestions of right and wrong behaviour were the guides to rapport. Kinsey himself carried out 7,000 interviews lasting an hour to an hour and a half. This labour of love was conducted deadpan; friendly, but never with any expression of surprise or disapproval.

The questions were asked as directly as possible to avoid interaction. The interviewer looked squarely at the subject and moved inexorably from factual background to intimate detail. Questions were fired rapidly, giving little time to think. Frank sexual terms were used. When abnormal behaviour was being probed it was "How many times?", not "Do you . . . ?" Questions were used to check others, husbands were checked against wives, reinterviewing after eighteen months was employed. This study is acknowledged as a classic. Its weaknesses are in its sampling rather than the method of interviewing. It is important, however, to remember that the questions were about actual sexual behaviour not attitudes towards it. The reports give little salacious pleasure and are a reliable guide for the same reasons.

WERE THE INTERVIEWERS TRAINED?

Kinsey and his three associates memorised the coding system of their interview schedules so that subjects saw only symbols being recorded. Most reputable research agencies have some form of selection and training programmes for their interviewers. The Government Social Survey uses only standardised, structured interviews. Because design is by experts and questions are piloted, the interviewers have to follow the wording of the schedules. Some latitude is allowed over factual questions, but with attitude questions there can be repetition but no alteration. Even prompts are written into the schedules and stock phrases are provided for probing obscure answers.[11]

Obviously with such care over design and such control over the interviewers, training is necessary. Moser reports that only 16 per cent of applicants finally passed all tests and went on to actual training in 1953.[12] Applicants are sent a handbook to study in advance and invited to attend a three day initial training class. Those accepted after this go into the field with a training officer who demonstrates the method and observes early attempts. If successful a probationary period is entered during which supervision is provided. Then a written test is given on the principles in the handbook. Trial interviews are recorded to check reliability. Even when fully trained and experienced there is still supervision by training officers. Once on the job these interviewers know how to approach subjects, how and where to sit, the tone of voice to use and the time to bring out the schedules.

Government Social Survey workers have to be particular because of the importance of the subject matter they handle. But this care illustrates the gap between the best and the worst. Many market research organisations have no selection procedures and little training. It is common to use students from social science departments both as training for them and as ways of gathering data for research. Anyone who has interviewed, canvassed or even tried to get factual information from strangers knows that the apparent incomprehension of many people is boundless. In addition the interaction can range from hostility, through indifference to seduction. Training at least alerts the innocent.

The success of training has been illustrated by Durbin and Stuart.[13] Here experienced Government Social Survey and experienced British Institute of Public Opinion interviewers were compared with another sample of inexperienced students. There was a striking and consistent difference in the proportion of schedules that were successfully completed. The experienced got more filled in, received fewer refusals, and reported fewer "gone away".

HOW MUCH CONTROL?

The Government Social Survey exercises rigid control over its interviewers. Kinsey and colleagues adjusted questions to suit the subjects. A solitary interviewer like Zweig sees his work as always a pilot study, always open to the importance of the chance remark to follow up.[14] Questions are varied between subjects and the aim is to produce an informal relaxed relationship. To Zweig interviewing must be a two-way traffic. His own description of his technique highlights spontaneity, curiosity and joyfulness. He claims that he rarely gets refusals, partly because of his classless foreign accent. Zweig's work may not be reliable but he has pioneered some important issues later recognised as such by social scientists who have employed more systematic techniques. There is a place for both the pioneer and the settler.

While insight or reliability might be legitimate objectives, it is often difficult to find any description of the conditions of interviewing in published accounts. Where none is given it may be safer to assume that little trouble was taken to control the conditions for the interviews. Yet there are techniques available apart from careful training. Coding can be reduced to simple signs to avoid long pauses. Tape and video recorders can be used, enabling the interview to be checked later on by a second judge. Most subjects rapidly forget a tape recorder is present and cassette machines are inconspicuous.

Finally it is best to be cautious about results from interviews produced by a single researcher. Here the obvious danger is that by tone of voice, anticipatory gestures or some other action that Clever Hans as well as humans skilled in giving and interpreting cues could recognise, the eager researcher will get the answers he wants. Checks by second parties, the use of neutral interviewers can help. At least there should be some cautionary remarks to warn the lay reader of the dangers of self-fulfilling interviews.

WHO WAS BEING INTERVIEWED?

It has already been suggested that interviewing within organisations might be affected by particular circumstances, making generalisations hazardous. But other groups are likely to respond to interviewers in ways that introduce bias. Rich has pointed to the authority of an adult when interviewing children.[15] The child will be likely to seize on an answer rather than telling the whole truth. To Holt, a child's response to teaching is usually a game to deceive by acting docile, looking attentive, acting silly and so on.[16] If skilled teachers are fooled, interviewers will have little chance of learning the game. This is especially the case with difficult questions where children are reluctant to answer "don't know" and will grab at any hints offered. Part of the skill of being a pupil is to be able to detect clues and give the answer the adult wants even though it was not understood. Another difficulty is in communication. To phrase questions in words understandable by children is difficult, and there is a tendency to try to overcome this by speaking to them as if they were rather dense foreigners, thus further increasing the artificiality of the situation and the motive of the child to play the game this apparently simple-minded interviewer wants.

Old people are similarly prone to grab at answers and to answer irrelevantly.[17] They are also liable to grab the interviewer and involve him in some personal gossip. The interviewer is often someone to talk to, or from whom to get advice or sympathy. The interviewer struggles to get his question in against the old person's attempt to introduce his own problems. The old, like the young, are not likely to tell the interviewer to push off but are likely to suck him into their own personal world. In these cases the danger in the impact of everyday and scientific constructions of reality is that the former will engulf the latter, leaving the interviewer with the job of making some sense of the data in his terms once he has escaped from his subject.

Controversy 4
Is the initial teaching alphabet better than the traditional?[1]

The difficulty of using experimental methods to produce decisive evidence about everyday as distinct from contrived situations is common in education, where the usual experimental design is to take two groups, matched as far as possible or allocated to learning groups at random, and then to teach one in a new way to test the efficiency of this method against traditional means. If all the factors were controlled or randomised bar the methods of teaching, and this was clearly defined and put into operation, the results should show conclusively how successful the new method had been with the experimental group compared with that in the control group. The continuing controversy after many such experiments which have investigated the effects of streaming, selection, comprehensive schooling, new teaching methods and new curriculum, indicate how difficult adequate control or adequate randomisation is when human subjects are involved.

The Reading Research Unit at the Institute of Education, University of London, has organised two major studies of the effectiveness of i.t.a.[2] In their scope and control they are not typical, and the care taken in designing the experiments makes them a model of their kind. Basically they are examples of the most common form of experiment in education, depending on two matched groups being tested after being exposed to two different forms of teaching. Because the design is that used in the simplest experiment in natural science, these examples are very significant in showing how difficult it is to control adequately all the factors involved when the material being used and tested is human.

The first experiment started with children starting to learn to read in September 1961. The progress of the experiments was reported as it went along because of the practical implications of the spread of the new method. Schools were added to the experiment as they decided to use i.t.a., so the number of schools and pupils in the reports tends to vary. However, from 400 children in twenty schools in 1961 the experiment expanded to about 2,000 children in a hundred schools by 1963. The samples used were mostly over 500 and many were over 1,000.

The experiment involved matching trial and control schools according to location, size, pupil-teacher ratio, amenities, minimum age of entry and social class. Pupils were matched for age, sex, social class, measured intelligence and vocabulary. Teachers, like the schools in the experiment, were volunteers, choosing whether to use i.t.a. or traditional orthography (t.o.). In the classroom, the same *Janet and John* readers were used, being translated into i.t.a. in the trial schools. All teachers in trial and control schools attended a one-day course before starting, and there were equal numbers of evening meetings and visits by the research staff.

This design controlled most of the factors likely to produce differences in progress in reading. Yet Southgate, reviewing this research, while recognising it as the most reliable available, urged caution.[3] She warned of possible experimental effect as children and teachers felt the stimulus of being involved in an experiment. She pointed to the weakness of controls over the teachers, for they were not allocated to classes at random. Lastly there was an absence of standard practice in the classroom. These criticisms were anticipated by Downing and the Research Unit and a second similar control group experiment was started specifically to extend control over incidental variables that may have been affecting the results.

This second experiment started in 1963 and involved 1,100 children split into equal numbers using i.t.a. and t.o. in thirteen schools. The schools were matched as before, but this time classes were allocated at random to i.t.a. and t.o., not through volunteering.[4] The children were matched as before, but this time the same teachers taught the i.t.a. and t.o. They were asked to use the same methods and give the same time to both methods. The public were excluded as far as possible from the experimental classrooms. This gave more control over extraneous factors, particularly those connected with the enthusiasm of the teachers and possible experimental effect.

The difficulty of reaching conclusions based on this and other research arises primarily from the complexity of the factors that are known to need controlling and the ignorance of others that may be at work. Most of these control problems arise out of the confusion of medium and method: i.t.a. is a medium as is t.o., but each can be used in various methods of teaching to read and each teacher will be using her own unique method with her class. Teaching is a complex activity. The second Downing experiment above used the same teacher for both alphabets, but although this was the nearest to controlling the effect of teaching methods it may have left a set of very powerful factors to work differently within the experimental and control groups. Teachers may work harder on the new to make it work, or concentrate most energy on traditional methods to prove they had been right all the time. There is no way of knowing whether either or none of these possibilities occurred.

The i.t.a. development was remarkable, not only because it was a very radical suggestion, but because it was so rapidly and so thoroughly investigated. Yet the experiments have done little to take the heat out of the debate and neither lay public nor professional evaluators have agreed over the meaning of the results and the reliability of the methods used in the experiments. Yet the practical importance of the research in deciding whether the new alphabet should be widely used makes this a key practical example, for a new alphabet once adopted would make further change difficult. In 1965 the Schools Council decided to evaluate the i.t.a. and by the time this report by Warburton and Southgate was prepared in 1967 seventeen major researches had been reported and many more were in progress in Britain and abroad, including the studies by Downing reported earlier. Warburton and Southgate's evaluation of i.t.a. reviews the design of the various experiments and lists the possible weaknesses.[5] They asked thirty-six questions about each experiment. Yet their conclusions are guarded. While generally favourable in their evaluation of the new method they stress the need for even more research, not only to try to provide more reliable evidence, but to counter research organised by the sponsors of the i.t.a. It is this honesty about the prevalent use of research as a lever to exert influence as well as the thorough treatment of the problems of designing reliable methods that makes Warburton and Southgate's contribution so valuable.

The inconclusive outcome of all this effort is a warning of the limitations of existing research methods in providing answers that can be trusted as a basis of policy. Compared with many of the problems that researchers tackle, the task of evaluating a new method of teaching reading to young children would seem simple. Get two groups of children who are as near as possible identical in age, sex, ability and home background. Teach them in the same school by teachers having the same amount of time and resources, with one group using the new method, the others the old. Then measure the children's progress in learning to read on a standard reading test after enough time has elapsed. Here are none of the problems of what to measure, how to measure and how to get information on the people concerned that face most researchers. Yet with all the money behind this effort, there has been no conclusive answer.

It has already been suggested that the reasons for the inconclusive nature of the evidence has been due to the difficulties in achieving complete control of the many factors involved in teaching children to read and particularly the impossibility of separating the effects of medium and method. Furthermore there are so many ways of teaching reading to young children in operation that it is difficult to make any comparison. The Warburton and Southgate evaluation of i.t.a. contains comparisons in terms of earlier, faster, and superior, but without being able to say what is being tagged as later, slower and inferior.

However, absence of conclusive evidence has not stopped supporters and opposition claiming that this same evaluation confirms their position. In making these claims the cautions included by Warburton and Southgate are often left out or over-emphasised. One side leaves out the caution that i.t.a. was successful in the majority of schools, although not in all, and that any advantage may be lost after changing over to t.o. later on. The other side accentuates these possible weaknesses. In the correspondence following the publication of the report there was a tendency for both sides to assume that Warburton and Southgate had assessed the most effective way of actually using i.t.a. thus further extending the confusion of medium and method.

Anyone interested in the way in which innovations are generated and disseminated should study this correspondence and the whole history of i.t.a. Pitman himself, although a commercial publisher, has been honourably cautious. Supporters of rival systems have been strident. Associations have lined up on both sides. A former president of the Coca Cola Company of Canada left seven million dollars to the i.t.a. foundation for research.[6] Downing, has not only produced the most reliable experimental work but has been a powerful advocate for the new medium.[7] Other experimenters have complained that their work has been ignored. Yet all the resources of the National Foundation for Educational Research, the Ministry of Education and the Schools Council have failed to produce evidence that will give a simple answer. Like every issue involving people, there are too many factors at work for an experiment with sufficient control to provide results that are conclusive. The introduction of i.t.a. will depend on the strength of rival pressure groups rather than the status of the available evidence. All the controversies in this book confirm this inability of social science to provide decisive answers to crucial questions.

The base line from which experiments can be gauged consists of two situations identical except for the exposure of one to the factors which have been assumed to be causes of the changes that are anticipated. The simple control group experiments of elementary biology, with one gas jar with live beans alongside another with the same quantity of marbles, are of this type. If all factors bar those under investigation are under control through matching in experimental and control situation, it can be confidently assumed that the causes of any change are these experimental factors.

In the social sciences two groups can be similarly organised and the experimental group exposed to the factors assumed to be causal. But here the confidence that the experimental factors were the cause of the consequent differences between experimental and control group is lessened by the impossibility of controlling all the other possible intervening, extraneous factors, or indeed of even knowing which they are. Rigid control of humans either results in a synthetic situation or in an immoral one. It is possible to select a large sample and then divide it again at random into an experimental and a control group so that the unknown factors will be randomly distributed and likely to balance between the two groups, but there is no certainty. Furthermore, the causal factors such as home conditions, social class, streaming or the use of i.t.a. are themselves amalgams of many factors and as these are the ones not controlled, many extraneous influences will be present because of this weakness in definition.

Even in laboratory experiments there are genetic differences that can be controlled only by using identical twins and varied personal histories which are beyond control, yet influence perception and motivation. No matched humans can approach those well-scrubbed gas jars side by side on the bench. Early criminology optimistically developed on bigger and better control group studies, but all the sophistication in matching of delinquents and non-delinquents led to nothing conclusive and by the 1970s this method seems to have been abandoned.[1] Indeed, contemporary criminologists not only reject this attempt to find the causes of criminality but maintain that this was the wrong question to start with. All the effort devoted to matching might have been better spent asking why some actions and some persons are labelled criminal but not others.

Controversy 4 on the i.t.a. and Controversy 6 on de-streaming are other examples of the limitations of control group experiments. Here natural situations were used, so the matching would be imperfect and many crucial factors in the learning situations were not controlled. But all experiments with humans are situations of interaction with the continuous exchange of subtle clues that elude control. The rest of this chapter will be concerned with the improvisations, deviations and idiosyncrasies of experimenters and their subjects. The experimenter influences his subjects as he arranges the setting of the experiment, just as they attract or repel him. In these unusual conditions humans are at their most sensitive, suspicious and elusive. There are no less suitable subjects for experiment.

EXPERIMENTAL EFFECT

The effect of being involved in an experiment was first observed in the studies of the Hawthorne works of the General Electric Company in Chicago between 1924 and 1927.[2] These studies, initially concerned with productivity, were organised by Mayo at the Harvard Graduate School of Business and have been responsible for a shift in emphasis within industrial psychology. They have also provided the foundations for the human relations school of management. The reason for the lasting influence of these studies despite criticisms of their design will be discussed later.[3] Their importance here is in the detection of the impact of being involved in an experiment on the workers in the factory. After experimental manipulation of the material conditions of work it was concluded that productivity depended primarily on the human relations involved and that the interest shown in the workers by the experimenters was the main factor behind their extra efforts. Indeed, even the deliberate worsening of material conditions of work seems to have resulted in extra production due to the worker's feeling of being of concern to someone in authority. While these assumptions have been challenged on political as well as methodological grounds, the actual impact on the subjects of experimentation has been repeatedly confirmed.

This is often referred to as Hawthorne, or experimental effect. People under observation do not behave normally, but respond to the experimental conditions. The Hawthorne workers responded in a way that defeated the original purpose of the experiment and initiated a series of further investigations into the human relations that were influencing productivity and turnover of labour. An extraneous variable, initially unrecognised and therefore uncontrolled, had intervened and in many cases proved more influential than the variable of physical environment originally being manipulated. Experiments on humans are always subject to this effect which, if not controlled, may bias results.

One example of this can be seen in a recent experiment designed to involve parents in the affairs of a school to see if this improved the attainment of the children.[4] Children were tested for attainment before and after the experimental programme and in two other schools used as controls. However, the effect of the programme could not be compared with the control schools because these had reacted to the tests by drawing up new schemes of work, employing extra teachers and concentrating on improving the performance of the children on the tests. This unintended consequence of selecting schools for testing was named by the authors the Bethnal Green effect, after the Hawthorne effect that was the first indication of distortion caused by involvement in an experiment rather than by any impact of the selected variables. In the Bethnal Green case the effect was probably heightened by the status of the research directors. When notables and even university departments ask schools to join a project or experiment, Hawthorne effect is inevitable.

This effect has been demonstrated experimentally. As early as 1936 Canady, himself a black, showed how white and black children scored differently on intelligence tests when tested by white and black testers.[5] A white child tested first by a black and then by a white tester two or three weeks later gained I.Q. points. Black children tested first by black and then by a white tester dropped I.Q. points, despite the practice gained. Only in the 1960s was this type of study taken up again and there have been many confirmations that the colour of the tester makes a difference. Doubtless the current relations between the races is also an important factor.

Obviously if intelligence test scores are influenced by the interaction of tester and tested, personality tests will be even more vulnerable. One obvious influence would be sex and sex appeal. Rabin, Nelson and Clark arranged for males to wait in a room decorated with anatomical charts.[6] There was no difference when they were then tested by males or females. But a sample of men left waiting in a room decorated with pictures of nude women gave significantly more sexual responses to Rorschach ink blot when tested by men compared with women. While somewhat removed from general practice, this does indicate the importance of the sex of the tester. Furthermore, interpreting ink blots is hardly likely to arouse erotic feelings and other tasks might have produced even greater differences.

More reliable, if less enjoyable to take part in, was an experiment by Masling using eight postgraduate students to try out sentence completion projective techniques on two attractive female under-graduates.[7] These two women played warm and cold roles as they were tested. They had previously memorised two sets of responses to the sentence completion tests with equal numbers of sick and healthy responses. Their interactions with the testers were taped to check that their responses were the same with each tester. Each tester saw one of the girls in a cold and one in a warm role. They then wrote up their reports. Masling found that the testers made more positive statements about the girl who had acted warmly towards him and shown an interest in him than about the girl who acted cold.

This experimental check on the influence of a tester's response to the friendliness and sexual promise of the subject was also used by Masling to check scoring on the Wechsler-Bellevue intelligence test.[8] Here the warm subjects were scored more leniently, were given more opportunity to clarify or correct responses and were given more encouragement during the test.

However, experimental effect is only one type of unintended, uncontrolled effect on humans involved in an experiment. The observation of one person by another involves interaction, just as in the interview situation. Hence a two-way influence of experimenter on subject and subject on experimenter would be expected. Indeed, in the example above, the effect of being involved in a programme of testing under the auspices of Michael Young was enough to make the schools strive for the very improvement that was being tested. Furthermore, it has already been reported that experimenters can unconsciously affect the results of their experiments once they know the expected results. This applies as much to human subjects as to rats.

There is one other effect of being involved in an experiment that is important in assessing evidence from laboratory work. Orne has suggested that the fact of being involved in a psychological experiment is itself a source of influence on response.[9] Thus in experiments on hypnosis, Orne maintains that the setting itself gave the subjects a feeling of being part of an impressive, solemn experience that created effects that were impossible to separate from the hypnotic stimulus being used. They did their best to make the experiment succeed. Friedman has also pointed out that this confusion of experimenter and stimulus has always occurred in studies of hypnosis.[10] Mesmer himself must have credited his apparatus with powers of hypnosis that were actually his own. Mesmerism was confused with mechanically produced hypnosis. What experimenters do incidentally may be confused with the experimental stimulus they manipulate. It is necessary, therefore, to investigate, not only the effect of being involved in experimentation, but the effects introduced accidentally by the experimenter. This is another hole in the controls.

EXPERIMENTER EFFECT

In the ideal experiment there are simply subject and stimulus under the control of, but not influenced by, an experimenter. But in experiments with humans, interaction is inevitable. The researcher cannot remain neutral however hard he tries to standardise his actions. He greets the subjects, settles them down, varies his words, gestures and expressions, just as they vary theirs. In Goffman's terms, there is inevitably role distancing.[11] The experimenter steps out of his role to become interested in a pretty girl, to put a shy person at ease, to stop a child crying or comfort an old lady. In doing so he is breaching his controls over himself and making himself a factor in the experiment. He is giving clues to his subjects through which they can interpret the situation and get an idea of how to respond.

Rosenthal, in his book *Experimenter Effects in Behavioural Research*,[12] provides plentiful evidence of such extraneous variables, including his own experiments devised to test the effect on results of the expectations of the experimenter. In this work there is no indication of how these expectations were communicated to the subjects, but the process may be similar to that described previously where the owners of clever animals or mind readers managed to convey the requisite answer. If this is the case it is particularly relevant for experiments in education, for children in school are prepared to look for clues about correct answers.

Rosenthal and Jacobson, in *Pygmalion in the Classroom*,[13] describe a striking experiment to illustrate how teacher's expectations of children's performance can be established without any real evidence, yet can somehow be used to bring the performance up to that expected. The argument against streaming in English schools has rested on a similar argument that there is a self-fulfilling effect in education, whereby a teacher first labels a child, then treats him according to the label, until the child comes to behave in the way which the label describes. To Rosenthal and Jacobson teachers are Pygmalions because they too have expectations which serve as a model for moulding children. The implications for researchers in education are profound, for this influence may produce just the results the experimenter expects or even wants.

Oak School was situated in a poor area with a below average record of achievement. In the spring of 1964 all children were tested on a test labelled the "Harvard Test of Inflected Acquisition", which the teachers were told was a measure of academic spurting or blooming. In reality this was only an ordinary non-verbal test of intelligence; 20 per cent of the children in the school were designated "spurters" just before the teachers met them for the new school year. Each teacher in each of the three streams of each year was given the names of those children who should bloom accidentally. In reality this 20 per cent had been selected by the use of random numbers and any difference between them and the others was in the mind of the teachers alone.

At the end of the school year, the children were given the same test. Those who had been designated as "bloomers" among the younger children showed remarkable gains in I.Q., one in two gaining 20 points I.Q. in the experimental group compared with one in five in the control group. The gains on reasoning were even greater among the experimental group. When teachers expected children to spurt academically, they somehow made sure that they did. The self-fulfilling hypothesis applied here as it did to psychology students timing rats learning to run a maze. The most dramatic success was with younger children and there was little effect among those in the top two forms of this elementary school. There was no difference in the effect between different streams and little difference between the sexes. Later work has confirmed

99

that the expectations of teachers can influence not only academic progress, but motor skills.

There is, however, an ironic tailpiece to this experiment. In 1968 when *Pygmalion in the Classroom* was published attacks on its reliability were already appearing in the journals. Claiborn, in a replication of the experiment found no gains by the supposed "bloomers" and teachers seemed to be resistant to expectancy statements.[14] Rosenthal, the virtuoso in detecting experimenter effects seems to have been detected introducing some himself. But this is also an example of a book based on a small experiment, boosted by peripheral supporting material and combining data to give an impression of maximum certainty. Yet the book was freely available, while the articles were only to be found in academic journals. Those inside the discipline were equivocal and informed. Those outside were unlikely to have access to the sources of doubt.

Friedman, working with Rosenthal, gives a clue to the way influence is exerted. He filmed twenty-nine experimenters at work with eighty-six subjects on a perception test to see if uncontrolled influences were at work.[15] Observers then saw the films and filled in scales of the number of glances and smiles passing between experimenters and subject, another relating to the dress of the experimenter and noted whether he was wearing glasses or not. The behaviour of each experimenter was then related to the results of the experiment. The first result was that the experimenters behaved very differently. The second was that the way the experimenter behaved was an influence on how the subject answered. The exchange of glances and the time taken over the parts of the experiment were particularly influential.

Thus experiments differ in the degree to which they are controlled and a written account of the arrangements may leave out many uncontrolled influences arising out of the behaviour of the experimenter and his interaction with the subjects of the experiment. In a world in which the experimenter has an aura of professionalism that tends to impress, subjects are liable to over-cooperate. Orne has pointed particularly at the college student who appears as the subject of many experiments and who may be motivated to support a hypothesis, skilled at guessing what it is from the nature of the experiment and alert to the clues that the experimenter may provide about the answers that are needed for success.[16] Like many people in doctor's surgeries, subjects in a laboratory are keen to be good co-operative patients.

The key to successful and reliable experiment is therefore a sufficient level of control. There are three areas that need controlling, the subjects, the stimuli, and, from what has just been discussed, the experimenter and the environment of which he forms a part. Likely personality and background differences of the subjects can be controlled by having control groups matched as near as possible in all but the particular characteristic being investigated or through the random selection of groups. The stimulus can be controlled by careful definition, design and the elimination of all other possible influential stimuli. The behaviour of the experimenter can be controlled by standardising his actions as rigidly as possible. But from what has already been said, complete control is impossible in the behavioural sciences, because humans are so adept at obtaining meanings from apparently slight clues.

In the social sciences the most usual experiment takes the present situation as the effect of some past event and then traces back to establish a relation between the two. This is a popular way of bringing some scientific control in the investigation of important live issues.

But the degree of control over the many variables involved tends to be small. It would be interesting to trace the education of successful people to see if factors such as attending public or progressive schools were important. But education is not definable as a single factor and many other influences will have been at work. It may be possible to match groups to eliminate the effect of some of these extraneous factors, but reliability is likely to be low and alternative explanations for the present situation being investigated cannot be eliminated. History, politics, economics and sociology abound with the resulting controversies between rival schools of thought, all claiming support from analysis after the event.

The major obstacle in any *ex post facto* explanation is that the causes indicated could never have been used to predict the event. Everyone theorises about the causes of crime or war by examining past events, but none of the combinations of factors suggested as the cause exhausts all the possible combinations. These explanations are plausible only because the event has already occurred. Such experiments are always inadequate. Different people will choose different factors and give each factor a different weight in the explanation.

THE FOLLOW-UP STUDY

In education and criminology it has been common to trace the development of selected groups across the years. Successive measures are taken at different ages and the last measure serves as a base line for the next. Large numbers are needed to allow for losses from the original sample over the years of the study. In theory a control group is needed as a check on the experiences of the experimental group, but these have rarely been included.

The most common way of selecting a sample in education has been to take all the children from an area born within a limited period. Sampling discrepancies still arise. Some children at the lower end of the intelligence range will inevitably be excluded. Where a group with some particular characteristic is chosen the chance of a biased sample is increased. Thus Terman followed a group of highly intelligent children for twenty-five years to check their physical, intellectual and personal traits to see what sort of adults they would become.[17] This has been an influential study, but later critics have shown a weakness in the way Terman selected his superior group.[18] Out of 1,758 superior children that he should have located, only 643 became the test sample. These were chosen because of performance on a verbal test of intelligence and consequently overlooked those whose intelligence manifested itself in other ways. Hughes and Converse have argued that if the

63 per cent of non-responders had been included, very different results would have occurred. As many of those not included were under-achievers and maladjusted whose potential was not reflected on test results, a complete sample may have shown that highly intelligent children have more, not less, school and personality problems than average.

The most ambitious British follow up study has been directed by Douglas.[19] This involved 5,000 children born in March 1946 and produced fifty-two articles and books by 1968. The subjects range from breast-feeding, bedwetting and circumcision, through application for places at Oxbridge to the development of pubic hair and genitalia. The most influential of these studies has been *The Home and School*, published in 1964. But criticisms of this book have been serious. Burt has pointed out that the work depended on a number of tests which were only assumed to measure the qualities assessed.[20] Furthermore these tests were given to eight-year-olds on the assumption that they were capable of giving reliable answers. They were also administered by teachers without experience of this type of work.

The second criticism was directed at the changes in test scores between the ages of eight and eleven years. There were no attempts to show whether the differences were statistically significant and Burt produces evidence to show that differences in the tests at the different ages could have accounted for any difference in performance. Burt's third criticism was of the way the results were interpreted to demonstrate a large wastage of ability due to selection for secondary schooling. To Burt, Douglas is claiming that his tests, given by inexperienced teachers to eight-year-olds, are indicators superior to the actual selection procedures themselves, carried out only a few months before selection. But even the figures presented in *The Home and School* could be interpreted to mean that innate ability was being fulfilled by selective secondary schooling. Burt does not press this case, he presents it as just as plausible as the interpretation presented by Douglas.

Horobin, Oldman and Bytheway have produced a more specific criticism of *The Home and the School*, related to the widening gap between the measured ability of children in different social classes as they got older.[21] Their conclusions, like those of Burt were that divergencies in performance between the classes may have been due to different development of the children, but may equally have been due to the tests used. There was no way of telling whether the apparently widening gap between the social classes in their performance on tests was due to a genuine divergence or to the method of statistical analysis. Horobin, Oldman and Bytheway report evidence from a follow-up study in Aberdeen to show that no widening gap occurred when different tests and different methods were used.

The basis of this criticism is that the tests must be capable of being described in terms that are independent of the age of the children to be tested. But any test for one age range is inevitably qualitatively different from any test designed for another age group. The ability measured on the first test may not be the same as that measured on another later on. Furthermore, the difference in performance on the two tests is in part due to a recognition of a development in ability with age that has been built into the test. Thus the results of children taking different ages are a compound of the effects of ageing and of the tests. The apparent widening of the gap between middle-class and working-class children in measured ability as they get older may therefore be due only to the type of statistical analysis used.

Horobin, Oldman and Bytheway argue that there is evidence to support the theory that class differentials in measured ability are present at all ages rather than gradually widening. This means that children from different social classes initially scoring the same on a test cannot have their changes in scores on later tests compared directly. The criticism applies not only to the data on the widening gap in measured ability, but also to the evidence presented by Douglas on the effects of streaming.

Controversy 5
The Reformation and the schools

The controversy that follows is taken from history. It illustrates not only how different selections of evidence can be used to support different causes, but how the same evidence can be used to reinforce or undermine a cause by reporting it within a different context.

Towards the end of the nineteenth century A.F. Leach, working for the Charity Commissioners as they tried to sort out the affairs of the endowed schools, produced a number of articles and books that changed existing ideas on the history of English schools.[1] Leach worked from the surviving records of the Chantry Commissioners and challenged the accepted view that the grammar schools originated at the Reformation. Indeed he favoured the idea that the Reformation was a disaster for education, destroying the grammar and eliminating the elementary schools. By going back to the original sources he appeared to have corrected a mistaken view of the history of schooling. Partly as a result of this work, Leach was chosen to write or edit the chapters on schools in the *Victoria County Histories*.

While there had been adverse criticism of Leach, the first attack using other documentary evidence came with two articles by Mrs J. Simon in 1955. These criticisms were repeated in her book *Education and Society in Tudor England* published in 1966.[2] Simon's criticisms of Leach were that he lacked historical perspective and artificially abstracted the history of the schools from the general history of the period. In particular he suppressed or ignored evidence that countered his opinions. Consequently Leach overestimated school provision before the Reformation.

Simon also suggests that Leach held these views as part of his involvement with the Charity Commissioners in adapting the surviving endowments to form a new system of secondary schools in the late Victorian period.

A vigorous defence of Leach was published in 1963.[3] In this, Chaplin maintained that Simon's criticisms, like many others, were derived from original criticisms forty years before. Furthermore, in his defence of Leach against Simon, there was also an attack on work by Jordan[4] which had seemed to further weaken Leach's argument. Jordan's massive analysis of English philanthropy in the fifteenth and sixteenth centuries built up a strong case for this period as the real starting point of English secondary education on a large scale. But Chaplin argued that Jordan had been influenced by Simon in his views and had misjudged the real evidence presented by Leach. Indeed, despite the criticisms of Leach by Jordan, he still relied on the evidence collected by Leach although, according to Chaplin, not always acknowledging his debt.

The final twist in this controversy can be found in criticisms of the work of Jordan himself. Curiously these mainly concentrate on the very criticisms that Simon had originally levelled against Leach, for Jordan, in making his detailed tabulations of bequests across nearly two centuries ignored accompanying economic changes. Among these changes the most crucial was a fall in the value of money. Fisher has calculated that had this been taken into account, an apparent dramatic increase in philanthropic aid to schools in the period after the Reformation may have actually been a fall.[5]

These controversies over the use of documents and their interpretation illustrate the difficulties of reaching agreement when the historian can select among the material available and when fresh documentary evidence is liable to be found. The importance of these controversies is not that they show how the political attitudes of the writers affect their use of documents, but that one view often comes to be accepted without sufficient evidence. Once accepted it becomes dogma, unquestioned unless fresh documentary evidence becomes available or there is such a change in the political climate that research guided by new views on old problems is stimulated.

Documents and other unobtrusive 8
measures

Most books are not based on information gathered for the purpose but are collections of material, often first published in articles, that has been organised by the author to present a new perspective on an issue. Thus articles usually rest on primary sources of data, books on secondary sources and later books on tertiary material from earlier ones. At each step, distance from the original study lends a misleading enchantment to the reliability of the primary source. The original article may have a cautious section on methods, the first book briefly mentions them and later ones just quote the evidence, not how it was obtained. Thus tentative suggestions may become hard facts.

This tendency for doubts about reliability to diminish with distance from the original investigation is also present when information is derived from documents produced originally for other purposes. Such documents are the main source of data for historians, but are also used by social scientists. In theses presented for higher degrees, a "previous research" section is used to show, not only that the student has been reading, but that the thesis builds on past studies. But documentary evidence is also important in providing a convenient way of finding supporting data for that obtained by the sort of methods so far discussed. The more methods that are used, the more checks there are on the reliability of the results. The frequent stress on the necessity for students to "do research" by touting round questionnaires often obscures the rich sources already available in libraries and various records.

The assessment of evidence derived from documents requires

the same three basic questions to be answered as with all forms of research. The test of reliability is still whether another researcher would extract the same information from the available documents. There is still a need to assess whether enough care has been taken to ensure that superfluous information has not been taken as central. Finally the extent to which the information that has been extracted can be generalised has to be determined. Reliability and validity are still central issues.

Gottschalk, reviewing the use of personal documents in history selects as the first problem for the historian the establishment of the authenticity of the document.[1] Secondly, if the document is reliable, the credibility of the evidence in it has to be determined. The historian adopts the attitude of the lawyer towards evidence, questioning the ultimate source of the evidence, the ability and honesty of the witness and the accuracy with which he has been reported in the document. Finally he looks for corroboration by independent sources. Thirdly, the historian has to assess the relevance of the information. It is useful historically only if it relates to other history rather than standing as an isolated incident, however interesting.

Thus Gottschalk is asking whether the text is genuine, and if so, what is it really saying. However, while all users of documents should be concerned with their reliability and validity, the historian has his own conceptual framework and methods of investigation that alert him to the need for caution. The historian is trained to reconstruct past events by reference to their specific place and time. The historian's use of documents is grounded within this context. Social scientists, concerned more with change than with concrete events, use documents more freely. But the absence of reference to a particular time and place and the absence of training in using documents in the social sciences often results in uncritical use. Historians spend lifetimes in establishing the authenticity of documents. Others seize them without thought as convenient grist to their mill.

There are two major difficulties in using existing information in documents. First, the definitions and categories may have been adequate for their original purpose, but not for the social scientist. Secondly, information in documents may be used as an index of a concept, but the fit between them may be dubious. This can be illustrated in criminology where the number of documents relating to offences committed, the nature of the offenders and the disposal of those found guilty suggests a rich fund for research.[2] There are annual reports of the Commissioners of Prisons, the annual report of the Council for Central After-Care Association, the annual report of the Commissioner of Police of the Metropolis, the irregular reports of the Children's Department, Home Office and above all, the *Criminal Statistics for England and Wales* published annually as a blue book six months after the close of the year to which it refers. This seems to be documentary evidence at its most reliable.

Yet this collection of apparent riches cannot even satisfactorily show whether crime is increasing and certainly does not provide an adequate index of existing criminality. This weakness is concealed beneath the deceptive simplicity and certainty of the mass of figures and tables provided. The root of the trouble lies in the initial collection by different groups of person for different purposes using different definitions. *Criminals Statistics* is a collection of reports from chief constables, but these depend on harassed policemen and clerks of courts fitting cases into legally defined categories as best they can.

This legal classification also gives no information about the circumstances of the crime. The weakness in the link between the statistics is in the existence of crimes that are either unknown to the police, ignored by them, or not cleared up. There is no way of knowing how large this figure is compared with those cases that do appear in the statistics. Indeed, an improvement in police efficiency, by reducing this dark figure and inhibiting criminals may actually reduce the level of crime, but would show in official statistics as a crime wave.

Secondly, the number of offences in each category depends on current police practice, which is itself influenced by current attitudes towards particular sorts of crime. Sometimes this is a deliberate change in procedure. Thus in 1931 there were 26,000 property offences in the Metropolitan area, but this increased to 83,000 in 1932, because the "Suspected Stolen Book" was abolished and all cases went into one category.[3] Sometimes discrepancies result from pressures on the police to stamp down on a particular offence. Any such changes in procedure will produce large fluctuations in crime because the offences known to the police are only a small part of the total.

The situation is confused further by the lack of any connection between the three sets of statistics: offences known to the police, persons found guilty in the courts, and offences cleared up. Furthermore there is no way of knowing whether the offences were committed by first offenders or hardened criminals. Thus in 1965 there were 292 offences of blackmail cleared up and 179 persons prosecuted. But there was no way of knowing whether these were 179 prosecutions for first offences with the rest cleared up without prosecution, or fewer persons prosecuted for two or more offences and so on.[4]

Moreover, even if these anomalies could be sorted out, the statistics would remain unreliable.[5] Behind criminal statistics are not only overworked clerks doing their best to classify crimes correctly, but a legal system that cannot ensure the proper use of definitions and often aggravates statistical bias by inappropriate definition. The police are reluctant to offend certain prostitutes and homosexuals because they act as important sources of information. The public will not report crimes if they think the law is unfair. Thus prohibition in the United States was almost universally broken.

Above all, criminal statistics give an impression divorced from reality. Policemen have scarce resources. They concentrate these where they seem to be most needed. This usually means concentrating in working-class areas or where business property has to be protected. The police do not usually concern themselves with fiddling of income tax and other white-collar crimes. They are also wary of excessive zeal in pursing traffic offences which might jeopardise public relations. Within the police system, too, procedures are necessarily arbitrary and imprecise. The author, while station constable in the police, once refused to listen to a woman who complained four times in one week about being assaulted by her boyfriend. The fifth time she encountered a more sympathetic ear and action was taken which resulted in a three-year prison sentence for the man concerned. It is on such chances that statistics are built.

To Cicourel, official statistics of juvenile crime are made up in the same way as rumour is generated and transmitted.[6] Vague and discontinuous pieces of information are transformed into ordered occurrences. A written report is prepared that is rounded and simplified to fit the case into the standardised categories of the bureaucratised procedures of justice. A clear picture, not only of the crime, but of the criminal is established through the use of contemporary ideas about causation in delinquency. The police interpret calls, assign men, screen reports, establish routine, label people and fit them into categories. They create histories out of available clues. In doing so they process people into standard types of criminal and, as part of this, into a part of criminal statistics. Bureaucracy conceals individuality under statistics and creates convenient fictions of predictability. Thus criminal statistics should not be used as indices of the state of crime but as indices of how delinquents are processed.[7]

From this picture of the processing of delinquents the weakness of criminal statistics can be seen. They represent a simplification into legal categories accomplished through the actions of many hard-pressed officials working according to procedures established within their various offices. But the same process lies behind many apparently neat sets of figures. Furthermore, this process not only applies to statistics compiled by officials, but to those gathered by researchers. To Cicourel the basic question about all information is its relation to the original acts that it represents, indicates or measures. The answers to an interviewer or on a questionnaire, just like the figures in a table of statistics, may not be accurate descriptions of reality, but gross oversimplifications. The researcher uses contemporary theories about delinquency, achievement, ability, opportunities or environmental influences to shape his report in a form that is convincing to a reader.

To Cicourel the crucial test would be if these interpretations of observations, questionnaires or interviews were defended before an audience who had access to the original documents. He uses the example of an investigator presenting his account of what happened in an event to an audience that had access to video tapes of that event. Immediately the meaning of words, gestures and actions would be in dispute. The policeman, the teacher and the researcher are all engaged in simplifying, objectifying and categorising; the reader only gets their version of the events. It is very likely that access to information that lies behind the written account would produce violent disagreements. Yet such an opportunity is rarely given. Official statistics are usually taken to be reliable indices of the state of actual affairs and the results presented in research reports are rarely accompanied by enough information for the reader to see how the final simplified statistical picture has been produced. All tables and rates conceal and distort reality. Most have been produced by slotting the cases into the nearest category, rather than into one which actually fitted the particular circumstances. In the case of courts, prisons, hospitals, school records, police statistics, government offices and surveys, there are routines for producing the figures in the tables that simplify classification by processing each case into the available categories. The consistent rates that often emerge may be the result of steady, predictable human behaviour. They are as likely to be the result of consistent practices within the organizations producing the figures. It may be, as Cicourel has argued, that the focus of research should be on the labelling and categorising process rather than on the figures themselves.[8]

We can now return to the study of Polish peasants by Thomas and Znaniecki.[9] Not only is this a classic study using the analysis of documents but it has also been subjected to a thorough retrospective evaluation. The authors were concerned with the problems of social change and particularly of immigration. They adopted the viewpoint that such a study, as in all sociology, was necessarily concerned with the way individuals interpreted the situations they were in as well as with the circumstances themselves. Because there was this emphasis on the importance of subjective factors, personal documents were selected as the source of materials for analysis. These were assumed to reveal individual attitudes to events.

The documents used included letters, autobiographies, newspapers, court records and records of social agencies.[10] There was no clear account in the book of the way these materials were obtained. The letters seem to have been bought after an advertisement had been placed in a Polish émigré journal published in North America. The newspapers were bought in Poland by Thomas while on a visit. Documents were collected from an agency concerned with emigration from Poland. There were records from émigré Polish societies in America and court records from areas around Chicago with large Polish populations. Finally there was a long autobiography by a Pole who had only recently left his native land. Blumer, assessing the reliability of these documents as sources from which a picture of a changing society could be drawn, concluded that they were inadequate.[11] They were fragmentary, discontinuous, leaving gaps that had to be filled in through the knowledge and imagination of the authors. The letters which formed the bulk of the documentary evidence gave no picture of the background or living conditions of the writers. The picture presented in the book was drawn by the authors, interpreting the material and filling in the gaps from their own knowledge of Polish life. Thomas himself admitted that he and Znaniecki were "indisputably in the wrong" to give the impression that the theories in the book were founded on the data.

This problem of interpretation applied also to the remaining documents. Records of courts or societies, newspapers and life histories had to be interpreted and to Blumer the interpretations that were made were not obvious from the material and in some cases the interpretations that were made were devious and even naïve. Similarly the autobiography could have been interpreted in a number of ways and did not even seem to reflect the genuine views of its author. Furthermore, there was no way in which the reader could judge whether Thomas and Znaniecki's interpretations were correct. All that was clear was that these interpretations were blended together to give a consistent total picture, but one that was drawn by the authors. There was no way of assessing whether this overall picture was valid or whether individual items contributing to it had been interpreted in the way the original author intended.

To Blumer the use of documents as a source of investigating attitudes raises a fundamental dilemma in the social sciences.[12] It is necessary to investigate the meaning people attach to events as well as to study the events themselves. Yet attitudes are elusive things to measure. Personal documents may be indispensable as sources for detecting attitudes, but they do not stand up to the three tests used here. They are open to different interpretations by different readers, they are uncontrolled because they are written freely for non-scientific purposes and they are the work of an individual and therefore not necessarily representative.

Thomas and Znaniecki's study is unique in depending on human documents to develop a theory of social change and in its exposure to critical assessment and defence after a period of twenty years in which it had established itself as a classic. This exercise has served to confirm the difficulties of using documents, even where they are specially written or are contemporary with the events being investigated. There are three sets of interpretations at work to reduce their dependability. The original writer does his best to give meaning to his situation and to communicate his views. The writers who collect and analyse his letter, life history or description then have to write their own account and interpretation. Finally the reader has to decide what this version means. This process may be taken further as later writers use the book or article, interpret and often condense it for another generation of readers. At each stage there is another set of interpretations and further opportunities for introducing bias.

The analysis of documents need not, however, rely on the uncontrolled interpretations of the researcher. There are methods of content analysis that are both objective and systematic. There are explicit rules and procedures that limit the freedom of the researcher to exercise his own judgment over how to categorise and how to decide on what to include or exclude. Thus the reliability of this technique can be high.

UNOBTRUSIVE MEASURES

The advantage of documents as sources of evidence is that they have been compiled for other purposes than to provide information for social scientists or historians. They can be assumed to be a reflection of feelings undisturbed by the presence of the researcher. This is also the case with other traces of activity. Humans leave evidence of their activities around, and alert social scientists can use this source to build up a picture of natural behaviour. Webb and others have produced a book on such sources.[13] They range from counting the liquor bottles in dustbins to measuring the wear on carpets in museums.

Mass Observation was a typical unobtrusive means of collecting information on normal behaviour on such days as the Coronation of King George V on 12 May 1937.[14] Some thousand observers noted anything that interested them, details of overheard conversation, striking local events, the weather and the response of people to the event. Similar day-surveys have left a record of normal routines, contacts, feelings and impressions. The observers were a very articulate, and mildly radical group. There was no control over their observations. The accounts are still vivid but have all the weaknesses of inductive methods. With no guidance from any hypothesis or definition of issue or population to be observed, there is little that could be a springboard for later work.

In practice, unobtrusive measures probably play an important if accidental part in most research. The social scientist going about his everyday activities is alerted to the behaviour of others by the discipline he practises. As he drinks his beer in the pub, squeezes into the tube train or sits in the cinema he takes in the scene with an eye skilled in fitting casual observations into the orderly model in his mind. As he gets involved in planning a research project these models are sensitive to relevant perceptions so that his hunches emerge from a combination of theorising and casual observation.

As interest deepens in a subject alongside the organisation of research, newspapers, journals, radio and TV become sources of information. The researcher interested in curriculum change starts to view school timetables systematically. Those investigating loneliness in old age find new interests in the reading rooms of public libraries, railway station waiting rooms and park seats. Births, marriages and deaths columns in newspapers are perused by those interested in social networks among the middle classes.

Few of these measures are sufficient by themselves to provide reliable data. But they are an important confirmatory source unaffected by the researcher. They can add both insight into and actual measures of human behaviour. Their limitations are those already suggested for all documents, plus the often unsystematic way in which the evidence has accumulated or has to be collected. Nevertheless such measures are probably an important and neglected source of evidence, avoiding many of the snags associated with research involving obtrusion into human activity.

This is an appropriate point at which to close these chapters on research techniques. No single technique is necessarily superior to any other. What is certain is that they all have shortcomings and if used alone are unlikely to give dependable results. This points to the importance of triangulation, the use of multiple methods. The ideal investigation employs a variety of theoretical perspectives, a number of researchers, different research techniques and an assortment of samples. This ensures that the final results will not be the product of one fallible researcher, using one theoretical perspective and one method of data collection. A quick sortie with a questionnaire among students can produce results for rapid publication but equally rapid redundancy. Multiple, cross-checking methods are time-consuming but may have a greater chance of contributing results of lasting value.

Controversy 6
To stream or unstream?

This controversy illustrates the difficulty of obtaining conclusive answers to practical problems through research, even where the design problems appear to be small. But it also shows how evidence can be interpreted to present a case which is more formidable than warranted.

In the 1930s streaming was introduced into most elementary schools. This grouping by ability was soon supported by evidence from educational psychology. The attack on streaming opened in the 1950s. This was part of a general attack on selection procedures, secondary organisation as well as streaming. It has been notable for the vigour and organisation of the parties involved. It soon stimulated a movement in defence of the established system, making it difficult for the lay reader, not knowing the allegiance of the writer, to judge the reliability of the evidence used. Only in 1970 was a large scale, adequately controlled and neutral investigation published.[1] It was predictably inconclusive.

The first campaign for de-streaming opened in the magazine *Forum*. De-streaming soon became a popular research topic. The first evidence came from Finch (1954),[2] Rudd (1956),[3] Blandford (1958),[4] Morris (1959)[5] and Daniels (1959).[6] Finch, Blandford and Daniels favoured de-streaming. Morris found streaming beneficial for the teaching of reading and Rudd detected little difference in the two methods. In 1959 Yates and Pidgeon from the neutral position of the National Foundation cautioned readers about drawing conclusions from these early and poorly controlled studies.[7]

The zenith of the reformers came in 1964. Forum held a

conference, submitted evidence to the Plowden committee and published a paperback, *Non-Streaming in the Junior School*.[8] In this year Douglas published *The Home and the School* reporting that streaming reinforced social selection within the schools.[9] Finally Jackson condemned streaming as discriminatory and unjust.[10] The shortcomings of the Douglas study have already been discussed. Jackson drew extensively on Daniels and used personal interpretation rather than detached investigation as a method.

Only after 1964 was the attitude of the teachers controlled in the experiments. In the Plowden Report streaming was shown to lead to higher attainment. De-streaming was favoured, but only if the attitudes of teachers and the organisation of learning were favourable. Finally in 1970 a major study for the National Foundation for Educational Research was published.[11] Here 5,500 children in seventy-two junior schools were studied. With the controls built into this research no clear conclusions were drawn. Given enthusiastic, skilful teachers, non-streaming had advantages, particularly for the motivation of children. But even in unstreamed schools about half the teachers still supported streaming. Increased control over this influence had here led to decreased certainty.

This tendency for reliability and certainty to be inversely proportional appears in all the major studies. In the U.S.A., not only is the most carefully controlled experiment inconclusive,[12] but a review of all available American research could also detect nothing definite.[13] In Sweden a summary of the available investigations suggested that streaming produced slightly better results in academic achievement.[14] Finally a review of evidence from many countries concluded that streaming could not be explained in solely educational terms, but was essentially a reflection of the organisation of society.[15] This review of international evidence also concluded that conclusive evidence was unlikely ever to be collected as the variables involved were too complicated for adequate control. The attitude of the teachers was the most important and the most difficult to control. It was also the link between the organisation of the society and the organisation of learning.

The failure to produce conclusive evidence over a method of organising schoolchildren where controlled experiment is possible and the subjects unlikely to distort the results deliberately indicates the limits of social scientific research as a reliable source for decision making. Few areas of research present such an apparently simple design problem. Yet the efforts of researchers in many countries to improve design to answer the question of streaming or non-streaming have only led to greater certainty that the results will be inconclusive.

This is not the impression given to students or the lay public. The research has been used as a weapon, not a flashlight. It took twenty years in England for a major study to be published after the start of a campaign backed by small-scale research. Excluding the cautious evidence of Douglas, the accounts appearing in books are heavily selective. Of all the small-scale studies, the most quoted is that of Daniels, which was also the most favourable towards de-streaming. Indeed, no other research has produced such strong evidence for the academic as well as the social benefits of de-streaming. This is the one higher degree thesis which is extensively quoted by students in examination answers. Yet this was only a pioneering study by an enthusiastic egalitarian of two pairs of junior schools with negligible controls. The conclusions about the brighter and duller children were inevitably based on very few children. It is significant that Daniels's study was chosen for replication by the Surrey Educational Research Association.[16] The report, published in 1968, came to the opposite conclusions. Here achievement in streamed schools was significantly higher. The same methods produced opposite results.

This failure to find any differences in attainment between children who had been in streamed classes compared with those who had been in unstreamed did not, however, disturb the confidence in research to come up with a conclusive comparison. A follow-up of the N.F.E.R. study two years later once again found no differences and this time the attitudes of teachers were not controlled.[17] But the response of critics was not to conclude that the available techniques were too blunt to measure differences, but to press for an extension of the research into middle and secondary schools.[18] Neither was there any increase in doubt among the de-streamers as the reliable yet inconclusive evidence accumulated. The cry for more research was still a reflection of the conviction that sooner or later evidence would catch up with faith. It is not enough to believe, it is necessary to support belief with figures.

Just as a researcher allows himself freedom to express his personal opinion over the meaning of his results within the limits set by his discipline, so this book, from this point drifts away into a more personal view. The polemic is serious, however, for it aims to alert the reader to the misleading way some evidence is presented due to the conventions established within social science.

Unfortunately the conventions of reporting scientific research reduce the chance of enough intelligible information being given to the layman to enable him to detect weaknesses. Didactic deadpan gives the impression that the Oracle has spoken. Only those inside the professional community are experienced at seeing behind the mask that is a scientific paper. The conventions conceal the real backstage nature of research. Moreover, there is not free communication between the different sciences. They speak different languages and rely on different journals, associations and conferences, partly to reinforce their own sense of community but also to mark themselves off from others.

STATISTICS AS A PROP

A comparison between government reports or private enquiries of today with those 150 years ago shows how far we have moved into an age of statistics. Education reports before 1950 contained few figures or tables. None was based on systematic, bespoke research. It is now common to publish major reports in two parts, one a report, the other a tabulation of statistical data. The balance of description to statistics in education varies from the Newsom

Report, *Half Our Future*, containing fifteen pages on the accompanying survey, to the Robbins report on higher education with 2,097 pages of evidence published in separate volumes.[1]

The mass of supporting statistics in contemporary reports is the swollen descendant of the efforts of the Benthamites in the 1830s to produce hard information on which to base new policies to cure new urban, industrial problems. The pioneer efforts of statistical societies in London and Manchester, of medical officers of health, of officials like Chadwick or of energetic citizens like Engels or Booth have blossomed into the principle that every opinion needs its reinforcement of figures to appear respectable. Simple, even non-mathematical, texts abound.[2] There are also many books and articles showing how statistics can be abused to distort. There are others detailing mistakes in the presentation.[3] There are even articles to help researchers to boost the appearance of reliability of their work.[4]

The need for caution over statistical presentation is illustrated in the use of the term "significance" and the use of significance levels. It is very impressive to read that the results are significant at the one or five per cent level. But this figure only indicates the possibility that the statistics presented have occurred through chance rather than through the existence of some genuine difference or association. The chance refers to the sample used. The one per cent level of significance means that there is only one chance in a hundred that the results were due to the particular sample that was used.

However, many writers have argued that significance tests are used in situations where they are inappropriate or even misleading. Labovitz, reviewing the evidence available to 1970, concluded that significance tests are not useful in social research and should be disregarded when they appear.[5] Writers on the use of such tests did not agree on areas where they were legitimate. Nine papers supported their use only where random sampling had been used. But Gold has argued that genuine random sampling is impossible.[6] Selvin's view is that they should be confined to experimental studies.[7] Similarly Coleman has argued that they are misleading in survey studies because they only give a measure of the possibility that results are due to chance whereas other factors may exist that would provide a better guide.[8] Camilleri maintains that they should only be used to test theories but not specific hypotheses.[9] There is no agreement. Uses seen as legitimate by one writer are rejected by others.

The persistence of significance tests in social science research in the face of such criticisms can be explained first by their apparent precision. Indeed, their use may actually obscure the presence of uncontrolled extraneous variables and accumulated bias. The tests have become an important convention of social science and every higher degree student feels the need to find room for some somewhere in his thesis. They give an appearance of certainty associated with the natural sciences. Above all they impress on the outsider and amateur the superiority of social science as a source of wisdom about important topical issues.

WORDS AS WINDOW DRESSING

The object of writing an account of research is to convey information with precision. If the readers are not fellow professionals this also requires the use of plain words. Yet economics, psychology and sociology were given by Gowers as examples of new disciplines using jargon.[10] The tendency of writers in the social sciences to be "jargantuan" is unfortunate, as these disciplines owe their expansion to their apparent relevance to problems that concern the lay public. But the real danger is that the use of complicated words, whether accidentally or intentionally, can attach a veneer of academic superiority to inferior material. A technical vocabulary is necessary for clarity and precision of meaning, but can also serve as a smokescreen.

The disasters are reports worded like the "Development of Educational Theory Derived from Three Educational Theory Models" submitted to the U.S. Office of Education, containing the information that "Storeputness is a system with inputness that is not fromputness".[11] The likely response to jargon can be gauged from the attitudes of teachers to research. Cane and Schroeder have shown how sensitive and annoyed teachers are with technical terms.[12] Southgate and Roberts, in a book to help teachers over the criteria for choosing a method of teaching reading, comment that none of the research has been reported in a manner that would allow teachers to comprehend and interpret it in the context of their jobs in the classroom.[13] Yet teachers are an educated minority interested in obtaining guidance from research evidence and the i.t.a. research has been written specially for teachers.

Sociology moved into the front line of this predicament as it seemed to offer perspectives on issues central to teachers and to be producing evidence about real problems. Most modern sociologists, of all schools, draw on terms developed by Talcott Parsons as he formulated grandiose theoretical systems. Despite the criticism of this "grand theory" and its obtuse language, it has become the private language of sociologists but the despair of the public.

This problem becomes apparent when examination papers are marked. Thus the work of Bernstein on language has produced a mass of misunderstandings and howlers. The belief that working-class children are linguistically all depraved, converse only in monosyllables and grunts, and never speak to their parents, while middle-class children are continually employing elaborate sintaxis in philosophical family discussions, springs from a desperate attempt to understand and reproduce this sophisticated theory. The alternatives are to use original articles written in an unbendingly difficult style or rely on potted versions. Even Lawton, in a useful attempt to produce a simplified account of this work confesses that there are parts which were not comprehensible to him.[14]

This is a central dilemma of an original thinker involved in developing a theory that has immediate relevance to thousands of teachers. It has already been stated that the dynamic of the research and the ideas behind it are not matched by rapid adjustments in popular accounts. This is partly the lag between the emergence of a new idea, its testing and the publication of the results in an academic journal. But this is followed by another lag before the new development is written up in a popular journal, accessible monograph or a book.[15] In Bernstein's case the lag appears to be about ten years. By 1970, when monographs on the work started to appear, ideas published in 1960 had become established in education. These ideas were therefore simultaneously misunderstood and out of date. Yet every new sophistication of the theory makes misunderstanding more likely and probably increases the reluctance of anyone to attempt a quick simplification for popular consumption.

The worst aspect of this communication problem is in the use of concepts that are originally a useful shorthand, but become a means of explanation that inhibits further research. The concept of delinquent subculture explains nothing, even where it is adequately defined, for real explanation lies in the reasons why subcultures form, persist and exert influence. Similarly terms such as achievement motivation, retroactive inhibition and cultural lag are useful ways of summarising a number of related ideas, but can easily appear to provide explanations in themselves. The more frequently such terms are used, the more danger there is of the public assuming that answers exist to key problems that have in reality barely been defined.

The lay reader is in the position of a shopper receiving the wrong change. The act was probably innocent, but a suspicious number of cases seem to favour the author. The professional can detect the catch. The lay reader is rarely in the position to recognise that he has been short-changed.

The first caution is over the words used to link the figures. The distortion here has come to be called the "fully-only" technique.[16] Differences are described as "fully" X per cent when the objective is to show a relationship, but "only" X per cent when the aim is to suggest that no relationship exists. There are many common variations on this ploy. "Twenty of the samples were selected for detailed study" usually means that the others did not look promising if the results were to confirm the hypothesis and were ignored. "Typical results are shown" probably means that the best were picked out. "Correct within an order of magnitude" may mean it was more wrong than right.

Another popular technique could be called stage army mobilisation. Here it is implied that the results presented are backed by all the other researchers who matter. "It has been long known that" may mean it has just been thought out. "It is generally believed that" may mean that a few others have speculated along the same line. "The results are in line with the major studies in this field" means that the point has been a matter of dispute. In some cases the mobilisation is predicted. "The need now is for further research", "Much additional work will now be required for full understanding" and "the research will continue as resources become available," all mean that the author does not understand the results, but is looking for a new grant to carry on trying.

Finally the written account can be wrapped up in the conventional language of science labelled by Watkins as didactic deadpan.[17] Scientists report their work in an impersonal, stylised manner that suppresses personal opinion and experience. Technical language is used to give the impression of absolutely reliable methods, unaffected by the personality and social life of the scientist involved. Scientists stage-manage the impression they give to their public.

REFERENCES FOR PRESTIGE

The legitimate use of references is to alert the reader to the existence of relevant work that illustrates and supports the point put forward by the author. It acts as a shorthand to those who share a discipline, summing up whole areas of evidence with a single name. First the references are selected to support a viewpoint and secondly they can become ends in themselves. An absence of references is suspicious, but so is a surfeit. The first possible misuse of references to look out for is over-abundance. When every line is littered with (Smith 1960) or (Brown 1961) the suspicion is that the author is boosting his case. The second misuse is the mobilisation of famous names to place the work on a par with the established. Dedicating the book to Hans, Talcott or Basil, writing it in memory of Bertrand, acknowledging a debt to Noam can serve the same function as a Soviet tribute to Stalin as the greatest scientist and Lysenko as his greatest disciple.

Such a muster of names also protects the author from criticism. Anyone on first name terms with the great and who acknowledges how much he owes to the advanced seminar at Harvard is unlikely to be the target of critical hatchet men. Furthermore, filling the work with references to the established increases the chance of getting it published as the referees used by journals and publishing firms will see no harm in further publicising their work. In a small specialism within a subject publishing its own journal, a few on the inside refer to each other while those trying to get in have to distribute their references diplomatically to get their work accepted. Oldcom found a correlation of 0.96 between footnote references to the chairman of the doctoral committee and the successful completion of 100 Ph.D. dissertations.[18] The reference is a neat way of combining flattery with erudition.

The second ploy is the use of the obscure and exotic. No one is likely to look up references to the *Revista Iberoamericana de Seguridad Social* and there are abstracting services which enable the author to find unlikely examples. Better still are references to unpublished Ph.D. theses in obscure foreign universities who are loath to let anything leave their archives. Another variation to look for is a concentration on long, foreign sounding names. Smith and Brown sound like amateurs compared with Raskolnikov and Skavar. The Vienna School is more impressive than the Department in Birmingham.

The third target should be the ingratiating truism. "As Kilroy has conclusively shown, orphans have no parents", is a model of many attempts to flatter. A fourth ploy to detect is the professional trump. Here the reference indicates to the reader that he does not share the company that the author keeps and therefore cannot challenge the written account. "Participants at the recent congress in Bokhara will confirm," neatly places the reader outside the jet-set Pale. Another variation is to refer to verbal communications or correspondence, preferably with some august academic. For the reader the healthy response is to ask what is being concealed by this deviousness, rather than any acceptance that truth has been revealed through contact with an oracle.

Extreme window-dressing in the form reported here is uncommon. However, the difference between lay and professional audiences produces a dilemma for all researchers and writers. An easy, simple style of reporting may reach a large audience, but not convey the complexity of the methods or results. Giving full technical details may restrict the audience to a small, sophisticated circle.

This dilemma can be seen in Cane and Schroeder's study, *The Teacher and Research.*[19] Here teachers' opinions on educational research were collected. Three-quarters of the teachers never saw the *British Journal of Educational Psychology* or *Educational Research*. They were opposed to the use of technical jargon, statistical tables and theorising. They even felt that Schools Council publications, written specially for teachers, were too complicated. Yet while demanding simplicity, these teachers were aware that potted, simplified reports left out the detail that was necessary for assessment of reliability and validity.

This report by Cane and Schroeder confirms the need for a more widespread knowledge of the status of evidence derived from research. The teachers suspected that values were mixed up with the research. They guessed that samples were often inadequate and unrepresentative. They detected that extraneous variables could have often accounted for results. They were suspicious of generalisations. What was missing was any systematic knowledge of the process of assessment. Without it the tendency was to reject all research rather than sorting out the good from the poor.

Controversy 7
How prejudiced are the British?

Investigating the relations between racial groups in Britain has rightly been a major occupation of social scientists. But as Moore has argued, the concentration on a social problem and the publication of evidence for purely pragmatic reasons, nevertheless involves putting forward a particular view of society.[1] Most of the researchers have assumed the desirability of social homogeneity, value-consensus and freedom from conflict. They have designed their surveys to measure the extent to which these ideals are being realised. In doing so they have tended to ignore the historical, comparative and sociological context of race relations. As a consequence, the interpretation of the descriptive evidence has been as varied and conflicting as the political views of those involved in the debate.

There are two difficulties in interpreting descriptive studies. First, there is no baseline from which comparisons can be made. There is no standard for an unprejudiced population, or the prejudice to be expected in a class-ridden or classless society. Any figure of the proportions which seem prejudiced can be interpreted as satisfactory or outrageous according to the values held by the interpreter. Second, the questions asked may have no relation to the social structure within which race relations are determined. It may be that beliefs about race are only reflections of class consciousness. It may be that discrimination against minorities is only part of a social structure based on the domination of one class by another. It may be that race relations can be seen only as an index of the extent to which minorities are integrated into a society of plural value systems and fluid groups. But surveys without theoretical reference cannot give an answer.

In the late summer of 1958 the first race riots on any scale took place in Nottingham and Notting Hill. This not only brought the worries over increased immigration into the open, but raised the question whether the British were prejudiced against coloured people. In the ten years that followed there were seven major attempts to measure attitudes on racial issues, culminating in the study conducted in 1968 by Research Services Limited for the Institute of Race Relations as part of its study on *Colour and Citizenship*.[2] The report of this study, running to 800 pages, has been described as a "royal commission", set up by the Institute of Race Relations and financed by the Nuffield Foundation.

At a conference on Race Relations of the British Sociological Association held shortly before publication, the need for the evidence the report would contain became clear for none available was adequate. It was favourably reviewed after publication, but only when it was referred to as policy-oriented research at its best[3] did critics attack those parts of it relating to the attitudes of the public and which were based on a social survey. The result of the ensuing debate over the status of the evidence leaves the problem of the level of racial prejudice in Britain as open as ever.[4]

The survey for the Institute of Race Relations was recommended by a group of social scientists acting as advisers to the Study of Race Relations. The field work was done between December 1966 and April 1967. The sample consisted of 2,500 white adults divided equally between Lambeth, Ealing, Wolverhampton, Nottingham and Bradford. Another 2,250 whites were interviewed as a control group, using a more limited range of questions than those used with the experimental group. The questions were designed to place those interviewed along a scale of attitudes ranging from highly prejudiced to tolerant, through intermediate points of prejudice-inclined and tolerant-inclined.

The major criticisms were directed at this scale for measuring tolerance.[5] First the book mentions four key and ten supplementary questions that formed this scale, but only contains the four crucial ones. Second, critics maintained that four items could only produce a crude scale. Third, the scale was criticised as containing three out of four questions concerned with housing and with having a built-in bias towards tolerance. Fourth, the scale was criticised as incapable of discriminating between the majority who fell between extreme tolerance and prejudice. The authors were indeed very cautious about treating the three-quarters who were prejudice-inclined or tolerant-inclined as distinct groups. Fifth, the questions were criticised as too long, one of the four consisting of twenty-seven words. Sixth, there seemed to have been no testing of the reliability or validity of the scale.

The reply made by Abrams of Research Services Limited, who contributed the criticised chapter, was that the compression of the original chapter from 20,000 to 14,000 words accounted for the lack of information from which the reliability of the evidence could be assessed and for the omission of the complete questionnaire.[6] The power of the scale to discriminate and the presentation of the results were defended as suitable for a book designed for the general reader.

Finally, the critics, in replies to Abram's defence of the survey, reaffirmed their criticism and commented on the inadequacy of his defence.[7] The point was made that if the scale was constructed as Abrams maintained, the book was misleading and contained contradictory statements about its construction. The second point was made that the survey was terribly misleading in lumping as tolerant many people of different degrees of prejudice, including some who may have been very prejudiced but who could not have been detected by this scale.

This debate ranged over only one of the thirty-three chapters in the book. Yet this chapter is crucial as it is the one that depends on a specially designed survey. The results are used to make comparisons with other survey results and to outline the attitudes of the British public on a range of key issues concerning the housing, employment and mobility of immigrants and their relation with white adults. The book was to provide a basis for informed policy decisions. Yet the one part that was concerned with apparently hard facts was challenged as having a soft centre.

It was in the interpretation of these results that the real dispute occurred. Regardless of the technical standing of the research, publication was a signal for acrimony. There were those who saw the evidence as a sign of improving relations and of the fundamental decency of the British. Others saw the findings as yet another symptom of a class society dominated by capitalist values and the politics of coercion. Others dismissed them as irrelevant and a further sign of the impotence of social scientists to effect social change and do anything but help shore up a decaying system by providing convenient statistics.

The difficulty in assessing the relations between races in Britain can also be gauged from the debate between Rex and Moore in their study in Birmingham[8] and Davies and Taylor in Newcastle upon Tyne.[9] Rex and Moore in their book, *Race, Community and Conflict*, saw discrimination as forcing immigrants into neighbourhoods and into particular types of housing. Davies and Taylor in their article, 'Race, community and no conflict', found that immigrants were not forced into accepting certain types of housing but actually preferred and chose it. This controversy in letters to *New Society*[10] includes not only claims that evidence refutes the views of the other pair of authors but challenges to the reliability of the other study. The conclusion that can be drawn from this correspondence is a recurring one. Each pair of authors seems to have produced the results that their approach to their fieldwork dictated. Their interpretations of each other's work also seemed to have sprung from their different ideological viewpoints. Those who feel that the world is basically harmonious take comfort from evidence that simultaneously confirms the coercive nature of human relations for those holding a view of the world as a cockpit.

Although every stage of social investigation involves interpretation and evaluation it is in the final stage of analysis that there is most danger of the researcher introducing evidence that does not arise from the investigation and of drawing misleading conclusions. It is at this stage that possibilities can become conclusions and hypotheses elevated into laws.

INTERPRETATIONS WITHOUT DEFINITION

Hypotheses are meaningful only in relation to the theoretical frameworks from which they are derived and to which evidence collected to examine them is referred. But some hunches have little foundation in fact and flourish through faith. This applies to many of the controversies in this book. Comprehensive schooling, de-streaming, the i.t.a., the need for smaller classes, are supported because they appear of merit. Once exploratory studies have produced some supporting evidence the case is given the backing of science. Each hunch becomes the centre of an organisation committed to pushing its case. Conflicting evidence is ignored or explained away and pressure is exerted politically.

An example of a hypothesis being accepted as a copper-bottomed certainty, only to be shown as a colander under investigation, came at a conference to consider the claims of learning by discovery.[1] This was sponsored by Stanford University in 1965. The discussion ranged over the many different definitions in use. Each participant came with his own version. Some wanted to deal with the issue pragmatically, focused on the classroom, while others wanted to examine the available evidence without consideration of the use of the idea. Wittrock concluded that none of the claims made for the method had been substantiated and few had even been tested. Faith seemed the basis of belief. In the little experimental work that had been done, definition had been so loose that discovery as a means of learning could not be separated from being an end in itself. Lack of definition made it impossible to see what was being measured in the experiments.

This lack of definition makes control impossible. Experimental work on the relation between the volume of a gas, the pressnre exerted on it and its temperature depends on the use of standard units of measurement. This is also the basis for replication. But the units are not those in common use. The result of each researcher using his own definition gives a false impression of the evidence available. Between 1920 and 1960 there were eighty-three studies of teacher effectiveness carried out in the School of Education, University of Wisconsin.[2] These produced 183 measures of teacher effectiveness, but in a monograph written within this department summing up this effort, none were seen as satisfactory and every new investigation had used a fresh one. Little that was useable or reliable had been produced. Yet money had apparently been made available for forty years and showed no sign of drying up.

The absence of definition is actually an asset for the elevator of hunches. Rhetoric can be easily inserted into the text. Scientific jargon without scientific definition can facilitate easy transition from facts to persuasive evaluation. An author is a man with normal healthy prejudices, restrained only by the research techniques he has used and his ability to suppress his urge to persuade, convert or impress. It is safer to assume that the writer is guilty until he has proved himself innocent. The more important the theme, the more likely is it that values will be mixed up with evidence. The more dead pan the account, the more is the caution needed in interpretation.

The gap between the everyday use of the term intelligence and the operational definition used by the psychologists has already been noted in chapter 2. The operational definition of intelligence is what intelligence tests measure. These definitions are precise and measurable in terms of the behaviour under consideration. Similarly the sociologist's definition of social class is usually father's occupation, but each reader has his own definition. Furthermore, the sociologist may himself slip from his operational definition to discussing social class in a general way. This occurs particularly in the interpretive stage.

Some definitions become major theoretical issues. The concept of ideal type has exercised sociologists, baffled their students and flattened the lay reader. Ideal types are described as tools for analysis, as consistent, logical models built up by accentuating the salient features of an institution. They are deduced, synthesised as a shorthand for further analysis. They are not substantiated definitions or hypotheses. Given this collection of verbal defences the reader will probably just accept the superiority of the social scientist using it. Gaping holes have been shot through the use of this concept, yet the user can always reply that no concrete example was intended. It is immune from destruction on grounds of being misleading in practice, for it is not a description but a logical deduction, an impression, not a product of actual investigation. Contrary evidence cannot disturb it. Legitimately it can sustain conferences and fill examination papers but it is a slippery film across the window that separates lay and professional in sociology.

SELECTIVE INTERPRETATIONS

The most common bias in interpreting evidence comes from the selection for discussion of only such of the data as fits the hypothesis. This is difficult to detect, as written accounts rarely contain enough information to reveal such selectivity. A thesis contains the full account. A book based on it contains only that deemed saleable by the publisher. A 'reader' or summary removes what is left. What is removed is usually the technical sections on methods. This is why 'readers', digests and symposia are dangerous and why original sources are best. The latter contain the detail needed for full assessment, the former contain only the juicy but boned parts.

An example of progressive simplification can be found in the very influential and well-designed study of different styles of leadership by Lewin, Lippitt and White.[3] In most summaries of this work the superiority of the democratic style seems unquestionable. The original accounts by the authors are more cautious. But only in the fuller of these original accounts are there results that throw doubt on the performance of groups under democratic leaders. For example, some of the evidence suggests that if productivity is a priority, authoritarian leadership may be superior.[4] Again, in fuller accounts there are details of the results when groups were criticised by a hostile stranger. Democratic and *laissez-faire* groups seemed to be prone to vent their feelings on other groups. It could be argued that "wars" occur in frustrated democracies and that the best hope for peace among men lies in authoritarian regimes.[5]

Frequently the arguments between authors and reviewers or other critics revolve round this selectivity. The critics maintain that the evidence presented does not convince or that an alternative or conflicting explanation is possible. The author often replies that shortage of space meant that crucial evidence had to be left out. The criticism that the methods used and the evidence presented do not justify the conclusions made by the authors has occurred many times in this book. Piaget's studies of child development, the Authoritarian Personality research, *Colour and Citizenship*, Coleman's analysis of adolescent society, the follow-up of children by Douglas, the *Polish Peasant* by Thomas and Znaniecki and the historical work of Leach, Simon and Jordan have all been subjected to this criticism. Yet these were chosen because they were among the most influential and the most respected studies in education, history and the social sciences. Work not discussed here is probably more vulnerable.

The best advice to the reader is to watch the adjectives. If it is reported that there is a high association between social class and educational opportunity, or between wastage of ability and selection for secondary education, the question to ask is high compared with what. The amount of crime or immorality may be high, but it is doubtful if any other age has been more law-abiding or moral, and in any case it would be impossible to define the items or make any genuine comparisons. The writer is usually comparing his findings with some golden era in the past which has never actually existed, or with some contemporary fictional utopia. What the adjectives really reflect are the beliefs and hopes of the author, superimposed on his attempts to be objective.

A special form of selective interpretation frequently occurs while new theories are being developed. Illustrative data has to be borrowed in the absence of evidence collected specifically to verify the new theory. This borrowed data may only be used as illustration but can become the bulwark of a theory within which it was not defined.

This practice is almost inevitable where the theories do not lend themselves to direct verification but must depend for credibility on analogy and case studies. But the examples are interpreted to fit the new theory and alternative interpretations are always possible. In the end the theory stands on its ability to explain old situations in more illuminating ways. By this criterion, perspectives such as symbolic interaction or ethnomethodology are valuable. But the selectivity involved in their illustration and in their extension to institutions not specifically studied for illustration makes them more elastic than concrete.

Symbolic interaction, for example, has a long history within social psychology. The ability of humans to look at themselves objectively and to act on this self-analysis to exercise control over their interaction with others through the manipulation of symbols has been used with imagination to explain behaviour in such institutions as mental institutions, juvenile courts and prisons. All humans seem to play games with each other, presenting veneers, masks and ploys. But this insight is based on one interpretation of the symbolic interaction. Others are possible. You cannot prove such a theory, and its application to actual situations is always selective.

This can be illustrated in the current vogue for symbolic interaction in education. Teachers and children do seem to be playing a game with one another. There does seem to be bargaining. Both sides do seem to be managing the impression they are giving. But the content of these games, contracts and exchanges has to be interpreted by the observer. Those children may be acting attentive, may pretend to be docile and play at the answer game with the full co-operation of the conniving teacher. But there is no way of confirming this. They may actually be attentive or somnolent, actually be timid or suppressed volcanoes, be driven to answer or be caught up in the mystique of a spellbinding teacher. Symbolic interactionism brings insight and life to the sociology of education, but it is a perspective, and as such, open to conflicting interpretations. Life may be a game, but genuine responses are, at least, a possibility.

The danger of theory-building by analogy can be seen in the rise and fall of many discarded or discredited theories. Functionalism, the dominant sociological theory, was derived from biology and pressed the similarities between societies and organisms. This brought new insights into the nature of social life, but it also brought absurdities such as group minds, homeostatic principles and societal evolutions. The analogy is an important source of insight. It is not evidence that can confirm the truth of that insight. Other selections of analogies can be used to destroy what had seemed to be indestructible. Other interpretations can use the same analogy to illustrate a conflicting perspective.

FALLACIOUS INTERPRETATIONS

Investigations of behaviour in society can be carried on at different levels of theory, data collection and interpretation. At one extreme the researcher can deal with social systems, at the other with individuals. In between are a number of different levels where analysis is possible. The difficulty is to keep the theoretical stages that come before and after data collection and the type of evidence that is collected at the same level. Data collected from individuals may not be applicable to groups, neighbourhoods or say anything about a particular environment. Similarly, information on collective life may not be relevant to individual behaviour.

Aggregative fallacies occur when generalisations about individuals are made from measures of collective behaviour such as rates of crime, birth or migration. The theoretical model here is psychological but the data analysed refers to groups. Conclusions drawn about individuals from such collective data may be entirely spurious. Thus the concept of anomie may be defined as a state in which individual behaviour is not constrained by social norms. But the easiest data to collect are rates of crime, drug addiction, housing, education and other indices of social disorganisation. Using this evidence to draw conclusions about the state of individual minds may be misleading.

It has proved difficult to avoid aggregative fallacies while investigating the relation between education and environment. Thus Wiseman,[6] working on this problem, found an apparently inconsistent result wherein intelligence test scores were more influenced by the environment than were the scores on attainment tests. Wiseman acknowledged that this and many other studies by other authors arriving at similar results were probably due to an aggregative fallacy.[7] The tendency to collect information on schools, neighbourhoods or towns yet generalise about individual children is widespread. A theoretical model of the individual tends to be used, but the data is from groups. It is likely that the "Manchester" research for the Plowden Report suffered from this type of fallacy.

The reverse of aggregative fallacies occurs when information collected from individuals is used to generalise about social relationships. This is an individualistic or atomistic fallacy. Thus another common definition of anomie is social disorganisation. Evidence derived from individuals should not be used to draw conclusions about this social condition. Again the crucial point is the level of theory and data collection. Sociologists are apt to use a term like anomie as absence of constraint over individuals one moment and as social disorganisation the next. Psychologists use terms like environment without reference to the processes that relate it to the individuals involved. Unless the level of theoretical model, data collection and analysis is clearly defined and maintained, fallacies are likely.

This is an oversimplification of a complex problem. Thus Alker details eight fallacies that are possible in analysis.[8] Riley has added two more where, although the actual research fits the theoretical model, the analysis sticks so close to a single level that information necessary for full understanding is concealed.[9] Psychologistic fallacies occur where a researcher ignores facts about social groupings in explanation. Sociologistic fallacies occur where information on individuals is ignored. Thus psychologists have tended to ignore the uniformity and predictability of suicide rates while concentrating on individuals' states of mind, while sociologists have been contented to generalise from suicide rates and ignore the insights from studies of those who tried and failed.

The levels of analysis can also confuse. This often occurs when a concept such as role is used. Sociologically role is behaviour associated with a position, regardless of the individuals concerned. The sociologist is concerned with expectations, norms and the way these are arranged in organisations and groups. But the sociologist often slips to the psychological level to explain behaviour. At the psychological level role is treated, not as a function of a position within a social structure, but as an independent factor influencing the behaviour of individuals as they perform or anticipate performing the role. Slipping from the sociological to the psychological level is akin to moving from a dependent to an independent variable.

This shift in levels also occurs in the study of organisations and the roles of individuals within them.[10] Sociologists are concerned with the structure, but to explain the effect on the individuals concerned fall back on psychological concepts such as internalisation and alienation. Thus role is used by the sociologist as behaviour which individuals occupying a particular position feel constrained to follow. But to explain why individuals actually behave in a predictable, regular way there is a switch to explanation in terms of the effect of the role on behaviour. The focus is on the organisation and data is collected with this in mind. But the individual is linked to this organisation by assumptions about individual personality and behaviour. The consequence has often been a picture of men in organisations as passively responding to pressures rather than active and often disruptive participants.

DISEMBODIED INTERPRETATIONS

A second tendency is to produce evidence, but bye-pass it while interpreting. This is a common danger given the real nature of scientific endeavour. The researcher starts with a hunch and ends with a certainty. The evidence presented in between may, however, not provide an adequate link between them. This seems to have happened in Musgrove and Taylor's study, *Society and the Teacher's Role*.[11] Conclusions about the despotic nature of teachers, the exclusion of parental interests from schools and the need to cultivate, not eliminate charisma in teachers under training appear in a concluding chapter. Yet there is little apparent relation between these conclusions and the very useful evidence presented in the previous six chapters of the book.[12]

Similarly the immense labours of Jordan to trace the philanthropic efforts of English merchants and professional men after the Reformation have left a mass of valuable evidence.[13] But Jordan's conclusions about the extent and nature of this charity rest less on this evidence than on his assumptions. Despite the amount of evidence collected it is still confined mainly to the merchant and professional classes and largely ignores other forms of charity by other groups. Yet Jordan's conclusions refer to the whole English scene, though there is no adequate basis for such a generalisation.

A final example is Riesman's *The Lonely Crowd*,[14] a best seller in social science, half a million copies having been sold of the paperback version published in 1954.[15] Larrabee saw this popularity as a symptom of an urge to national self-analysis in the U.S.A. at this time. The personality types suggested as paramount in different historical periods have become part of the language of sociology. But there is doubt over the interpretation of contemporary life that was presented. Riesman and Glazer, looking back after eleven years, admitted that they had serious misgivings about their thesis even before publication but decided to go ahead.[16] They admitted overestimating the degree of social change and the links between character and society. They also admitted that their analysis was incomplete, leaving out particularly such factors as the distribution of power which they later saw was crucial in understanding contemporary America.

DECEPTIVE INTERPRETATIONS

A third and more serious but less common fault is to wrap up a slanted study in an academic package. Some idea of the ease with which research can be used to support a cause can be gained from the article published in 1961 by Wiggins and Schoeck, 'A profile of ageing: U.S.A.'[17] This appeared in the journal *Geriatrics* devoted to diseases and processes of ageing. In appearance it is a conventional, provisional report of a survey organised by two professors of sociology. The methods described are convincing. A sample of 1,492 old persons were probability-sampled from seventy-eight areas, stratified by sex, socio-economic level, residence and geographical division. The authors admit that non-whites were under-represented because of shortage of funds, but claim that each old person in the area sampled had an equal chance of being selected. A table shows that the sample was close in age distribution, marital status and religious reference to the national figure in the U.S. census.

Here is an apparently systematic survey. Yet the research had already become notorious after one of the authors had read a paper based on it to a conference of gerontologists in San Francisco a year before.[18] This notoriety and the scrutiny of the methods used to collect the data were the consequence of presenting results contradicting all the available evidence and the policy of the profession. The critics had the full support of their colleagues to investigate and criticise. In reality the research turned out to be highly suspect. The sampling had been loaded to produce a profile of the aged as generally in good health, energetically independent and secure within family and community bonds. Yet only through the furore caused by the original paper did the overloading of the sample with more wealthy old persons come to light.

There is irony in the publication in 1960 of a collection of articles by Wiggins and Schoeck under the title *Scientism and Values*.[19] This attacks the tendency in the social sciences to concentrate on building pseudoscientific models and on producing quantitative data at the expense of insight into real problems. Thus at the time when the authors were gathering together articles to expose the pretensions of social scientists, they were engaged in research that was designed so as to support the stand of the American Medical Association against free medical care for the aged.

Controversy 8
The priority given to reducing the size of school classes

One justification for controlled investigation is that commonly accepted 'facts' often turn out to be rather dubious. Numerous attempts to find the relation between class size and achievement in school have failed to confirm that there is any benefit to the child in belonging to a small class. Indeed, superficially at least, the evidence suggests that larger classes tend to contain children who achieve more than their apparently more favoured peers. Fleming, reviewing the available research, found that of thirty-five investigations, two concluded that small classes obtained superior results, eleven that large classes were superior and twenty showed no measurable difference.[1] Rossi reports that over 200 large-scale researches have, by and large, shown that class size has no effect on learning, with the possible exception of languages.[2]

Four recent studies have confirmed that the only measurable difference favours large classes as environments for learning. A large-scale study of achievement in mathematics carried out in ten countries and covering 132,775 pupils and 19,000 teachers found no apparent connection between class size and the level of mathematics achieved.[3] What indications there were suggested that countries with larger classes got better results. A study in London by Little and Russell found that children in large classes learned to read faster.[4] Morris, in a study for the National Foundation for Educational Research involving 8,197 pupils in sixty Kent primary schools, found that reading standards were better on average in larger classes.[5] Finally Davie using material from the National Child Development Study came to similar conclusions.[6] Here 92 per cent of the 17,000 children born in one week in 1958 were traced in 1965 and given a number of tests. The information gathered on their infant schooling showed that those in classes over forty-one tended to do better than those in classes of under thirty on the tests of reading, arithmetic and social adjustment.

The importance of the National Child Development Study material is that it controlled many of the factors that could have accounted for the apparently anomalous effects of class size. Researchers had been scrupulous in pointing to spurious factors that could have been producing the results. Large classes tended to be in large schools which tend to have higher average attainment. Poor readers are frequently placed in smaller classes to increase individual attention. However, Davie was able to control for school size, streaming, length of time in school, use of independent schools, nursery schooling, parental interest and sex of child. There may still have been other intervening factors. Larger classes may be in urban schools where attainment is higher. Larger classes may necessitate formal teaching which prepares children better for formal testing of attainment. It may be that teachers in small classes try informal methods yet have not the skill to do this efficiently. However, where evidence supports existing opinion, no such scrupulous examination of possible spurious factors is demanded. Here, where common sense and policy is denied, there is a search to explain away the results.

Despite the evidence on class size, a reduction in numbers remains top priority for the teacher's unions. Every year the Ministry reports on the fractional reduction of numbers per classroom. The evidence is ignored and replaced with a disembodied appeal to reason and common sense. In the Plowden Report the Committee was faced with their own survey that came up with the usual result that large classes seem to facilitate greater achievement.[7] Yet their conclusion was that reduction in class size should remain a priority. The means for reconciling this are illuminating. The researchers reluctantly confirmed their unfortunate findings despite their efforts to eliminate them through control over possible spurious factors. The Report mentions the results, but says these are outweighed by professional advice, public opinion and the example of other countries. The writers of the Report seemed to have used evidence only where it supported their views and explained it away where it opposed them. No other evidence on the effect of class size was considered at all. Part 1 of the Report seemed to bear no connection to the evidence in Part 2.

Davie and other researchers have stressed that there are reasons for reducing the size of classes other than to increase attainment. However, the evidence does make the high priority given to such a reduction suspect at a time of shortage of funds. Given the mass of evidence on the adverse effect of poor environment on attainment there is a good case for improving education by better housing, welfare services and pre-school education rather than training more teachers and building more classrooms. But this is heresy, even though the evidence that is available seems to support such a redistribution of scarce resources.

Generalisations are a shorthand that facilitates communication without excessive elaboration. Terms like American, social scientist, working-class and human are generalisations, but to spell out the characteristics of all those involved would bring social intercourse to an end. As with stereotyping, the tendency to generalise is convenient but dangerous. This book is littered with examples where a degree of homogeneity has been implied that is a travesty of reality.

Social scientists are liable to two extra temptations. First, they are often the only group with evidence that seems to bear on important topical issues. They are asked to comment and expected to produce the facts. The consequence can often be to treat facts as elastic. The second temptation is to extend the meaning of evidence during this stretching. The operational definition of social class is converted into one that fits the topic under debate and so on.

There is a continual temptation to generalise from inadequate and irrelevant evidence. Most social scientists are delivered from this temptation by the constraints exercised by the communities to which they belong. This is why writing a popular book or article involves a risk of loss of prestige among peers. But there are many writers who popularise social science from outside the discipline, free to generalise beyond limits that would be acceptable within academic life. In cutting through the mystery with which scientists surround themselves the populariser escapes the discipline as well.

The first possible faults to look for are generalisations that transcend the samples on which they are based. This can result from ignoring non-response and assuming that those who did reply represent those who did not. It has already been shown that this has sometimes meant discussing a majority using evidence from a minority. But it can also involve generalising from one class, or nation, or age group to others. Between 1915 and 1964, nineteen of thirty-two studies of sexual behaviour had used samples of students.[1] Yet students are not representative of the whole population, particularly in sexual behaviour. Kinsey titled his books *Sexual Behaviour in the Human Female* and *Sexual Behaviour in the Human Male*, although his samples were drawn from one small part of North America and his interest was confined to a very small part of this extensive subject. American gangs probably have little in common with their English counterpart and family life in East London among the working class in the late 1940s may have no resemblance to that elsewhere or even to the situation in Bethnal Green twenty years later once redevelopment and affluence have had their effect.

A related fault is to generalise from too small or too unrepresentative a sample. Thus the modest attempt by Jackson and Marsden to investigate the process whereby working-class children do succeed in a school system in which the odds are against them provided information on an important subject where none had existed before.[2] But the sample in this study consisted of only eighty-eight working-class children and a control group of ten from the middle class all from one northern industrial town. Later writers have drawn on this evidence to discuss working-class education because it is all that is available.

In the social sciences the rapid expansion of numbers and the demand from the public for comment on topical issues have combined for generalisations to outstrip evidence. The sequence is frequently not from theoretical model, to hypotheses, to investigation and then to generalisation, but direct from model to generalisation. There is a danger of many following new fashions while a few produce a little evidence, too late. Before the relation between social class and educational performance had been thoroughly investigated in the early 1960s there was a movement in the sociology of education towards generalising about the school, with very small bricks of evidence mortared with much guesswork. By 1970, as studies of the school were being published, the fashion had become the curriculum, with even fewer solid bricks between the mortar. At each stage jerry building increased. There was an unstable, inverted pyramid in which too much weight rested on too little original work. The proliferation of 'readers', digests and popularisations provided a convenient boost to the impression of solidity. New peripheral subjects such as curriculum theory are prone to this elaboration of unsubstantiated theory.

Overgeneralisation is often not the original researcher's fault. Thomas, looking back over twenty years at the influence of his work on *The Polish Peasant* confessed that he had developed an aversion to it because the methods and the data had been forgotten while certain theoretical conclusions for which there had originally been little foundation in the data remained popular and were reproduced regularly by other writers.[3] The original generalisation may have gone too far, but once the author's cautions had been pruned there was no limit to the generalisations of others.

An example of the tendency for results to be used with decreasing caution over time can be found in the *Colour and Citizenship* study.[4] The doubts about the scale used to measure attitudes on racial matters in the survey for this book were concentrated on the lack of discrimination in the three-quarters of the sample who were neither very tolerant nor very prejudiced. Yet the results of this survey are compared with those from six earlier studies. It is admitted that different questions were asked and different approaches made, yet trends are defined and conclusions drawn. In the size of its sample and the academic backing it received, this was probably the most reliable of the seven surveys used in the comparisons, yet the criticisms of it throw doubt on its power to discriminate. It is very unlikely that a comparison between different surveys, using different questions is comparing like with like. The results are discussed as if there were no doubt that they are measuring the same attitudes and the trends are analysed as if the measurements were both accurate and highly discriminating.

Original doubts have been lost in the decade that elapsed between asking the questions and using them to detect trends.

THE INFLUENCE ON POLICY

In 1968 federal expenditure on social scientific research in the U.S.A. was 333 million dollars.[5] Yet the search for successful uses of this research proved unrewarding. U.S. government attitudes towards the usefulness of social science research could be gauged by the fall from 24 to $3\frac{1}{2}$ per cent since 1938 in the proportion of federal funds for research given to these subjects.[6] In Britain as in the U.S., commissions are set up to examine crucial social issues without social scientists being represented. Yet it is rare for evidence from social science to be completely ignored in final reports. To those engaged in decision-making, social science appears to be an academic exercise of marginal use.

It is only when simple and usually commercial decisions are to be made that the social scientist is called on, usually as a technician. The reasons for this will be discussed in the final chapter. In commercial cases a client negotiates with a research agency for a job to be done within a specified price. The client expects a report that will help in decision-making. There is no interest in the vagaries of the research procedures used. A report is given pruned of false starts and blind alleys. The research agency is obliged to produce results, produce them on time and present them in a form that contains few ifs and buts. There is also the possibility, as suggested by Controversy 3, that the client will in some way indicate the results he hopes will be found and the agency will prove susceptible to these clues about the outcome that would be welcomed.

But in all social science there is a pressure to produce results and produce them in an unambiguous form. Foundations, departments and businesses giving money for research expect results as a sign that their money has been well spent. The continuation of research in a department and the employment of those involved depends on producing the goods. Yet certainty and clarity are often impossible in the messy arena of everyday life. The ambiguous results and imperfect methods are cleaned up for public consumption. In the research marketplace as elsewhere it is all things bright and beautiful that sell. The honest remain not only poor but unpublished.

The pressure to produce results can be illustrated by the Institute of Race Relations report *Colour and Citizenship* discussed earlier.[7] This was to have appeared as a series of studies with a summarising work by the directors of the whole study. But the furore caused by Enoch Powell's speeches on immigration persuaded Rose and Deakin to produce a report as quickly as possible as a corrective and a guide to policy makers. There is no attempt in this book to conceal that the object was to remedy the social evil caused by treating coloured citizens as inferior, and the evidence produced was seen as a way of creating a more healthy environment for race relations.

The pressure on researchers is increased when dealing with topics of immediate practical importance. Here the values of the researcher will be most likely to influence his work. Indeed, it is these values that often account for the choice of area for research. The researcher is likely to be friendly with others sharing his views. He will be exposed to the advice of interested parties. The publication of results will be followed by many competing parties using his results to prove their conflicting cases. The greater the relevance of the research topic the more difficult it is to remain objective and remain deaf to interested, partial advice. Yet it is in just these studies that detachment is essential. It is also where the reader needs to be most alert.

However, the major contribution of the social sciences is less to produce suitable evidence for decision making than to investigate the gap between assumptions about real situations and the reality itself. It is as a puncturing device that social science operates most effectively. This type of research into whether there is really equality of opportunity in education or really an equalisation of incomes or a diminution in social class differences due to affluence is also less dependent on scientific detachment. There can be little doubt that if the research into social class and educational opportunity had been carried out by convinced Fascists rather than convinced egalitarians the results would have been different. The evidence that was produced was reliable enough to convince. It sufficed to demolish the claim of equality of opportunity and opened the way for reforms and a fresh look at the effects of the 1944 Education Act after more than a decade had passed.

This success in demolishing established beliefs compared with the failure to provide conclusive evidence for or against such innovations as destreaming, comprehensive schooling or the i.t.a. is an indication of the blunt nature of social scientific research instruments. These can produce evidence powerful enough to show that things are not working as planned or hoped, but not precise enough to compare different methods of organisation, teaching or learning. Evidence can be produced to challenge and question but not to prove.

The acid test is probably the ability to predict. This is the essence of the scientific law. 'Given this combination of factors the following can be expected' is a statement that can rarely be made with confidence when humans are in the combination. At the time of writing economists could not predict the effect on the balance of payments of joining the Common Market. When prediction fails factors beyond human control are blamed. But these are the very stuff of social science, for these factors are human behaviour.

The following are probably the most reliable population predictions for the United Kingdom for the years between 2000 and 2010.

1938	Charles predicted between 18 and 32 million (Great Britain only).[8]
1947	Hubback predicted between 31 and 34 million.[9]
1949	Royal Commission on Population predicted between 41 and 42 million.[10]
1966	Central Statistical Office predicted 75 million.[11]
1969	Central Statistical Office predicted 68 million.[12]

These alarming fluctuations include a swing from dire warnings of a declining population to near panic about over-population. Charles in 1938 made a lowest estimate of population in England, Wales and Scotland for the year 2035 of only 5 million. If predictions in the early 1960s had gone to that year they would have been nearer 100 million. Yet the change in contraceptive habits was at this date starting yet another unpredicted change.

The consequences of these fluctuations have been tragic. The 1951 census included a sophisticated measure of housing need, which, like all its successors proved to be a gross under-estimate. In education the failure to spot that the rise in births in the mid-1950s was persisting enabled the Minister of Education to approve the introduction of a three-year training college course planned to do without any output of teachers in 1963 when the immediate postwar bulge had passed through the schools. In practice this proved a disaster for the primary schools, although a boon to the colleges. The passage of the postwar bulge through schools and higher education has been a continuing story of shortage of places. Even the sophisticated predictions of the Robbins Committee proved inadequate within five years.[13] Elsewhere a similar failure occurred. The 1957 Willink Committee forecast that there would be a falling demand for doctors and recommended a reduction in the intake of medical students.[14] The implementation of this policy strengthened the bargaining position of the doctors but left the Health Service undermanned. A similar situation occurred in predicting the demand for, and supply of, scientists.

In practice it might have been as profitable to guess rather than try to predict. The major failure was to stick to the economist's dogma that demand determines supply. In reality the provision of social services creates the demand but while this was seen as self-evident by those doing the job, it was only accepted by the relevant Government Minister in 1969.[15] Sometimes being immersed in statistics makes it difficult to see the obvious. Teachers and social workers knew there was a shortage of school places, houses, hospital beds and welfare services. The statistics were too convenient as excuses for doing too little, too late.

The best documented post-mortem on research which was designed as a guide to policy followed the publication of the report *Equality of Educational Opportunity* for the U.S. Office of Education.[16] Like many such reports it has been labelled by the name of one of its authors although it was produced by a team. This Coleman Report has received praise as a first-class description and powerful indictment of the present effectiveness of American schooling. Criticisms have focused on the analysis of the results, the crucial part in work designed to guide policy.[17]

These criticisms read like a summary of this book. Some concentrated on the non-response. Others probed errors in measurement. There was disquiet over the interpretation of information used in the analysis but not collected as part of the investigation. Most criticism, however, was levelled at the theoretical model employed by Coleman and at his statistical analysis. Even if the data collected in the survey was not affected by uncontrolled factors, the flaws in theory and inappropriate use of statistics seemed to make it an unreliable basis for policy making.

Coleman's reply to his critics was that they expected too much from a theoretical model.[18] Largely because they were not sociologists they did not realise that if such a complete model were available there would be no need for a policy document as the problems would have already been solved. Coleman also defended the report as meaningful and digestible for the body that commissioned the work. To Coleman the critics over-estimated the state of knowledge about achievement in schools and as a consequence over-estimated the degree to which sophisticated statistical techniques could be used.

A comment on critique and defence by a third party produced the familiar verdict of non-proven, stressing flaws not only in the original, but also in the criticisms.[19] The dilemma of policy makers is acute. This report covered an important issue in American education. It presented results requiring some knowledge of statistics. But the criticisms were highly technical. This is the common fate of policy-orientated research. If it is directed at a wide audience it is vulnerable to professional hatchet men. If it employs the full array of conceptual and analytical tools it may please the professionals but will mystify and annoy the policy makers. Either way criticism is inevitable. The layman will gouge it in the name of common sense, the professional will dissect it in the name of science. Furthermore, both attacks are legitimate for both clarity and reliability are essential if policy is to be soundly based.

Once a report is available policy makers tend to use it selectively. Results are used when they support the views of politicians and ignored when they do not. The Plowden Report on children and their primary schools is a good example.[20] The accompanying research seems to have been a handy means of reinforcing existing fashions in primary schooling. Where the evidence opposed or failed to support the recommendations it was ignored or described as inexplicable and opposed to common knowledge. The sequence is not consideration of evidence and then decision, but decision and then the muster of evidence. This makes the production of reliable evidence even more important. Politicians can always find some evidence to support even the most cavalier attitude.

The conclusion to be drawn from the fate of social scientific predictions is that there is little chance that complex topical problems are open to solution through available methods of research. It will be argued in the next chapter that such a role for social scientific research is mistaken anyway and derives from a false interpretation of the organisation of science. Even so, the evidence may still be the best available and may be better than guesswork.

Where the public image presented by social scientists has done harm is in those subjects such as education that use the available evidence but are outside the social scientific communities. Here the danger is that evidence will be accepted as valid and reliable because of the way it is popularly presented and that it will remain in use long after it has been relegated within the discipline that produced it. Thus the Rosenthal and Jacobson *Pygmalion in the Classroom*[21] evidence came into prominence in books on education just as the critical comments and replications were appearing in inaccessible American journals. Barber and Silver's[22] review of twenty-one studies indicating faulty design and interpretation and Claiborn's[23] failure to replicate both appeared within a year of the publication of *Pygmalion in the Classroom* in Britain. But three years later in 1971 they had still not appeared outside *Psychological Bulletin* and the *Journal of Educational Research*, and Pygmalion effects were all the rage in education courses.

This is a serious situation because freedom to adjust is limited. Once it is assumed that social science can provide the evidence to support educational policy and practice, it is open to sceptics to challenge any recommendations that do not have this backing. But to admit that the evidence may be unreliable after claiming that such evidence must be produced to support practice is to surrender the authority derived from this empiricist claim. Students who have been continually asked for proofs of their beliefs will feel let down if they are then told that the supporting evidence is unreliable. In the time available on education courses no sophisticated approach to social scientific methodology is possible. Yet without it the tendency is to accept without condition. To switch suddenly from this view to a sceptical one would be liable to devalue such courses. As it is, social science is a dubious ally and there are many other subjects in the same position as consumers without a full view of production.

It is at this point where use is made of the evidence produced through social scientific research that the limitations described in this book produce a crisis. Here the number of academic subjects and organisations of government and business using social scientific evidence increases and more and more programmes of academic, governmental and business work are justified by reference to this evidence. But it is also here that there is a tendency to decreasing confidence in this evidence as control over its production through research is increased. But this decreasing confidence comes around a decade earlier within the social sciences than among the users on the margin. Furthermore, this marginal position gives only an obscure view of the actual processes of research and enables those within the scientific communities to boost the impression of reliability of the evidence presented to the public.

But it is also this gap between private, professional practice and public image that makes it possible to sustain the closed nature of the scientific communities by socialising successive waves of students before they are accepted as professionals entitled to produce and publish through reputable academic journals. The books on how to do research, the readers stripped of methodological cautions, the textbooks giving a smoothed account of the relation of theory and practice, the closely supervised and formally written thesis and the need to get accepted by established senior members in order to obtain funds for research and acceptance of publications guarantees that the production of evidence is disciplined and that it is presented to the public in a way that preserves the mystery of the craft. The consequences of this socialisation, the reason for its establishment and the escape routes that have been recommended will be the subject of the next and final chapter. It is also a description of the existing scope and future possibilities of social science, for it will be argued that the public and academic acceptance of social science, achieved through the establishment of closed scientific communities, has been unnecessarily constrictive.

The theme of this book has been that in the roles adopted by social scientists, in the techniques they use and in the way they communicate their findings, there is a gap between actual practice and public image. The reasons for the existence of such a gap can be seen by examining the organisation of social science at three levels of activity:

1. Where the values of the scientist impinge on his work.
2. Where social scientists are organised into communities.
3. Where roles have to be adopted during research.

THE IMPACT OF VALUES

The first part of the model adopted by social scientists from natural science was of value-free activity. Truth was seen as the aim of the scientist and objectivity was seen as the stance which would lead towards it. This was a worthy aspiration but, as has been suggested in chapter 3, a misunderstanding of the actual scientific position. In practice scientists strive after truth, but in directions and within limits established by the communities within which they work. The true and the valuable are not absolute standards, but are related to current scientific belief and practice. Natural science is not value-free, but permeated with values that each scientist learns as he becomes a fully accepted practitioner, as well as with personal opinions.

The attack on the idea of value-free social science has been sustained and bitter. However, it has not only been resisted as an attack on the status of social science, but has rarely penetrated the screen between professional and layman. The dispute can be found in a polite form in academic journals and in bitter disputes at professional conferences, but the only public battle has been expressed as part of the student revolt, where swingeing attacks have been made on sociology in particular as imbued with bourgeois values and defensive attitudes.[1]

To Gouldner, the idea of value-free sociology is a group myth, a caste mark of the decorous.[2] It enables sociologists to be morally indifferent, to escape responsibility for the implications of their work and to escape from the world into academic security. To Mills it has enabled abstracted empiricism to dominate research activity so that sociologists can become fact-gatherers for administrators and can ignore important political issues.[3]

The consequences of the persistence of the value-free myth can be seen in the wasteful proliferation of elaborate analyses of dubious data from questionnaires churned out by computers, which, as Runciman has pointed out, have produced nothing comparable in importance to the insights of classical social theorists.[4] These empirical studies supporting the ceilings of archive rooms in university libraries are often studies of the attitudes of students, the applications of new statistical techniques and comparisons of unlikely subjects such as primary education in Pimlico and eastern Tasmania. Each has contributed little to the sum of knowledge or the truth, but has qualified its author for membership of his community of peers by showing that he has learned the necessary procedures of research and reporting.

Gouldner has stressed the importance of this issue as follows:

> The problem of value-free sociology has its most poignant implications for the social scientist in his role as educator. If sociologists ought not to express their personal views in the academic setting then how are students to be safeguarded against the unwitting influence of these values which shape the sociologist's selection of problems, his preferences for certain hypotheses or conceptual schemes, his neglect of others? For these are unavoidable and, in this sense, there is and can be no value-free sociology.[5]

Perhaps the most important aspect of this myth is that its

implementation by educators may be unwitting, but is nevertheless crucial in supporting the established structure of the sociological community, for the values passed over to students include the value-free myth itself.

The second impact of values comes in the selection and survival of evidence until it virtually becomes part of the mythology of a subject. The Hawthorne studies have wide currency in the social sciences and subjects using such evidence.[6] But the original work has been strongly criticised.[7] First, the conclusions on the superiority of good human relations over material conditions and monetary rewards do not seem related to the evidence produced. Second, the frailty of the evidence does not seem to justify the survival of the conclusions. The Hawthorne studies and the human relations movement they initiated were supports for, and were supported by, the prevailing climate of capitalism and democracy. Workers could be kept contented by democratic means.

A similar case is the Lewin, Lippitt and White experiments on different teaching climates.[8] Here the frequently reported results again support democratic leadership. But one of the original research workers has explained how he and his fellow students put their all into the democratic but not into the authoritarian or *laissez-faire* role.[9] They were experimenting while Hitler was still a menace. They were involved in a violently anti-authoritarian period. But this climate has survived and accounts for the selective survival reported earlier.

The frequency with which both these experiments appear in textbooks can be explained by the support they give to paramount values in our culture. Both studies were an outstanding contribution to the development of social science. They are more reliable than most. Their fragility is unfortunate, but the selective nature of their survival is even more disturbing.

THE ORGANISATION OF SOCIAL SCIENCE

It has been the recurring theme in this book that scientists are organised into communities with established structures for socialisation, social control, authority and communication. Rex has described the community structure of the social sciences as feudal.[10] The young seek the protection of established senior members after demonstrating their competence in the pointless empiricism reported in the last section. Recognition comes through the demonstration of competence and professionalism in solving problems chosen because they are soluble with existing techniques. Preferment comes through gaining the support and protection of a highly placed and preferably politically secure professor.

This picture of a feudal community must include the peasants as well as the lords and their squires. At the top of each discipline there are usually a number of specialists connected into an "invisible college" by informal as well as official communications. In psychology Garvey and Griffith[11] have estimated that the immediate audience for most articles in scientific journals is around 200. Each subject is divided up into specialisms with narrow ranges of interest. The small number forming the "invisible colleges" also depend on close informal contacts as they research.[12]

The academic journal serves as one important turnstile through which aspirants pass before gaining recognition and as a medium through which the established inform colleagues of their current work, learn of the activity of others and pick out likely prospects for patronage. Editorial policy is therefore crucial in the horizontal communication that links the elite in scientific communities. Whitley in a study of thirty-two British social science journals has shown that in only nine were all articles submitted to referees.[13] In over half the journals the editors made decisions about publication themselves or just consulted junior colleagues in their own departments. Only sixteen journals had regular panels of referees and in all cases the editor retained the right to make the final decision.

These journals were edited by older, established professors who depended on their personal contacts in selecting articles. These would also be the same heads of departments who make appointments, negotiate for staff within universities, for money from foundations, serve on committees of professional associations, travel widely, organise conferences and act as spokesmen for the community in relations with the public. Policy, preferment and power tend to be in the hands of few senior professionals. This is not the public image of scientific activity and organisation. But it is also an organisation for the minority, mainly in the universities. There is little evidence on the relation between this elite and the majority who depend on their work. Scientific communities are no different from others in being organised hierarchically. They are unusual and feudal in the extent of the separation between nobility and serf.

This is obviously a gross over-simplification. There are not clearly defined scientific communities but numbers of specialisms within shifting subject boundaries. These specialists may form "invisible colleges" but interests are likely to spread into other specialist fields of study. There is continual movement in and out of the central groups where research is organised and financed. Around the universities are a growing number of polytechnics and colleges with flourishing and productive social science departments. Nevertheless, around the centre consolidated by abundant formal and informal communications, there are numerous groups of students, teachers and workers in the field who are neither linked together, nor linked to the central elite.

It is the absence of adequate vertical communication that enables the mystique surrounding research to persist. *New Scientist* and *New Society* are British attempts to provide links between centre and periphery. But a journal like *New Society* contains only ill-informed gossip about happenings at the centre. Above all, the insulation of central elites is maintained by informal communications, by feudal organisation, by the conventions in reporting research in academic journals and by editorial policy.

THE RESEARCH ROLE

To Cherns the research role adopted in sociology is derived from a system that rewards publication regardless of usefulness.[14] It is the opinion of peers that matters and the fate of the evidence produced is of no further consequence once the article on which such opinion can be based has been accepted by the editor. This is no different in the natural sciences, but here there is an established body of applied scientists to put the evidence into use. In the social sciences this development role is missing and those who work in the field tend to have low academic prestige and no compensating high pay. Cherns is supporting the view expressed by Rex, Gouldner, Mills and all those critics of contemporary social science, and particularly sociology, who see it as having adopted an inappropriate and misleading model from natural science. Inappropriate because the social sciences lack the applied scientists to implement the pure research. Misleading because, as Rex has pointed out, the model adopted is itself pathological. It is a model of the professional, established, organised scientific community, with a secure career structure for those who conform and funds for research if clients can be satisfied that the work will benefit them. It is the model of what actually happens in science, not the ideal that scientists support as their public image.

All these authors also agree on the reason for the adoption of this communal structure. The value-free myth not only enabled the social sciences to claim parity with natural science but led to an established place in academic life. Significantly, while Gouldner writes of an academic truce whereby the social sciences were accepted on the tacit understanding that they would concentrate on perfecting techniques rather than on criticising existing practices, Rex writes in terms of a social contract bringing about a feudal structure within the social sciences to align them with others in the university. All these authors are pointing to the same process of establishment. Respectability and recognition have been obtained at the cost of the right to criticise and the right to mix academic and practical work.

This is not an attack on the ideal of objectivity. This is still at the heart of science. It is an attack on the adoption of the form of objectivity without consideration of its purpose. The danger is that the motions of scientific activity are gone through for their own sake. Insight and the understanding of crucial social issues take second place. The mystery of science is used to preserve a public image while the discipline is applied to teach new members to conform. This adoption of the scientific model outlined by Kuhn has also resulted in a comfortable detachment from real issues. The attacks by Chomsky on the immorality of detachment by social scientists in the contemporary American setting are similar in quality to the complaints by social workers and teachers that academics are too far above the battle.[15]

The attitude of scientists towards their public has been described as a combination of chauvinism, xenophobia and evangelism.[16] All these signify the importance to scientists of preserving their position against the amateur, the outsider and the uninitiated, and of spreading the influence of the subject over new generations. Conflict within the scientific community must not upset the orthodox version for public consumption.[17] The existence around the fringes of social science of many denominations of popularisers and cranks claiming scientific status means that there is a permanent state of siege. Because it is the collective wisdom of the scientific community that decides what is scientifically respectable or not, it is necessary to expose anyone giving an impression that his work has this seal of communal acceptance. The softer social sciences may be more permeable around the walls but the keep is still strongly guarded.

Summarising, it has been argued that there are two versions of the scientific role. One is an idealised account of the independent pioneer at the frontiers of knowledge that is preserved as a version for the public, but contrasts with actual practice which consists of work disciplined by the values and organisation of scientific communities. Social scientists have adopted both the public version and the private practice. But the differences between the subject matter of natural and social science and the absence of an established base in the organisations in which the latter could be used, has produced all the disadvantages, but none of the advantages, of this communal version. In copying the structure of natural science and the methods developed for the investigation of non-human subject matter, the social sciences have achieved respectability and successfully concealed the accompanying triviality.

THE ROLES OF SOCIAL SCIENTISTS

As a step towards defining the scope of social science it is necessary to drop the fiction of the social scientist. It is not only that there are differing disciplines and different schools within each, but that there are many roles that contribute to that of scientist. Some idea of the range of social scientific activity can be gauged from the roles that have been played.[18] It is not being suggested that these are exclusive roles. Every social scientist slips frequently from one to another. Every social scientist engages in each role. This is why all have to be considered. They may occasionally lack the discipline that is associated with science, but they are what social scientists actually do.

The theorist aims to gain insight through building frameworks of related concepts into models of human behaviour and inter-action. The clarification of concepts and analysis of their relation is a step towards a fuller understanding of social life. From these frameworks hypotheses are derived which can be tested. The results of this testing not only show the usefulness of the hypothesis but often suggest new directions for theory building. Evidence is meaningful only when it is related to theories. Facts are meaningful only in the theoretical disciplines to which they are related. This is why psychologists and sociologists battle over the meaning of intelligence, race and social class, for apparently the same evidence has a different meaning in each discipline. Thus evidence has meaning only when related to the theories which are its context and source.

The technician may work for a client to solve practical problems, or work to provide data within an academic discipline. This is the most visible role of the social scientist and the one that can degenerate into an exhibition of virtuosity for the sake of satisfying the criteria of competence necessary for acceptance and promotion within the scientific community. But this should not obscure the value of technical efficiency. Modern societies depend on the collection of information. Where efficiency is combined with a full, clear and honest account of the procedures used, the reader can obtain the best view of how social scientists obtain their information. Books satisfying such criteria are Schofield's *Sexual Behaviour of Young People*[19] or the Schools Council's *Young School Leavers*.[20] These are usual in design but unusual in the clarity of the description of research techniques.

The critic concentrates on the gap between ideal and practice. This can be directed towards issues inside his discipline. An example would be Gouldner's book on *The Coming Crisis of Western Sociology*.[21] But the critic also uses his discipline to examine shortcomings in society. An example would be Mills's *The Power Elite*.[22] But a social scientist like Mills combines criticism of his colleagues as part of his critique of the contemporary social condition. It is unfortunately rare for the critic to lay out his position in advance of his arguments. His selection of evidence will be biased as he aims to counter other selections that he sees as prejudiced. But the arguments for including the criticial writer as a contribution to a syllabus are powerful. If the educator cannot be value-free, then it is right that he includes the views of those who advance conflicting values. Only then do those who learn from him have a chance to assess the spectrum of views.

The activist carries his other roles into action. As critic in action he is attacking that which seems unjust or inefficient. It is not only the student rebel who objects to the detached stance of social scientists and calls for active intervention to remove injustices. It is also the position of Chomsky and supporters of social science such as Senator Fulbright.[23] Active intervention in events may not be a conventional scientific activity, but detachment can be equally unscientific if the pursuit of truth is the end and science the means. This is particularly the case if detachment means the neglect of problems that are vital but unpopular and unlikely to attract financial backing.

The applied social scientist can be found in government, social work, education, industry and international organisations. Here they not only use knowledge produced inside academic communities but collect much of the data on which academic work rests. This applied role is under-represented in many fields of planning and development where the contribution of social science is not reflected in the numbers employed.[24]

Most social science consists of some combination of these five roles. The combination that is genuinely scientific is a matter of debate. The traditional combination of empirical work guided by, and reflected back on, theory developed in the mainstream of a discipline can be found in such work as Rex and Moore's *Race, Community and Conflict*[25] or Brandis and Henderson's *Social Class Language and Communication*.[26] What is being rejected is the narrow definition of social science based on technical competence exercised within narrow community conventions. There is growing support for such an expanded view of social science. There are the long established objections to the 'rat-box philosophy' of measuring bits of behaviour and summing them to generalise about human functioning.[27] There is the pressure to mobilise scientists as a counter to military and industrial power. An empirical base is being provided by the sociology of science, reflecting on the organisation, ethics and procedures of science itself. These movements emphasise the roles of critic and activist and relate these to the need for theory focused on important contemporary issues.

THE SCOPE OF SOCIAL SCIENCE

This chapter can be summarised as an attack on scientism, the adoption of a restricted model of science to gain prestige and reinforce the impression of dependability. Inside social scientific communities there is self-criticism and a staggering variety of perspectives and procedures. The outsider is given an impression of final answers to crucial social issues resting on solid bases of reliable evidence. The insider knows that even where empirical evidence exists, it produces even more questions than solutions.

The plea to include a broader definition of social science for public consumption is not to ask for less research. The shortcomings outlined in this book are surrounded by much that is both valid and reliable. Even if evidence has to be received with caution, it is nevertheless the best, and often the only source of information about social life. Indeed, the rapid rise in interest in social science is an indication of the need for factual information in modern societies. Providing triangulated, mutually checking methods are used, the social scientist can produce useful information for policy-making.

The dangers of the restricted version of social science can be seen in the growing number of subjects borrowing scientific prestige through the inclusion of 'the psychology of', 'the sociology of' or 'the economics of', that have proliferated in subjects such as education, curriculum studies, domestic science, physical education, youth and community service. The multiplication of A levels and curriculum projects in social science, humanities and general studies are other signs of this growing periphery. But in these subjects it is often the teachers as well as the students who have restricted access to the production of the evidence they use. Neither is there time to examine the standing of the evidence. It is used on trust and the contributions of the theorist, critic and activist are often omitted.

The scope of social science lies in the combination of insight and controlled investigation that is science at its most productive. But it also lies in the fresh perspectives brought to bear on stale issues. Questions have to be asked before answers can be suggested and investigated. The danger of the outsider's position is that the distinction between speculation and evidence is obscured by the way social scientists publicise their work. The drive to improve research techniques within social science should be coupled with more honesty in reporting and more education for the public in becoming more effective Peeping Toms.

The exhilaration of social science is in the range of related concepts that can be employed in investigating social issues. Social science is a haven for the curious, the alert, the detached and the nonconformist. This makes it even more urgent for social scientific communities to exercise discipline over individuals presenting new evidence. But the relevance of social science also requires not mystery but clarity in the picture presented to the public. Candour is needed to promote informed scepticism instead of naïve acceptance or rejection. This book was written to promote such scepticism. It should have been read in that spirit.

References and further reading

CHAPTER 1. SCIENTIFIC ACTIVITY IN THEORY AND PRACTICE

1. K.R. Popper, *Conjectures and Refutations: Growth of Scientific Knowledge*, Basic Books, 1963.
2. T.S. Kuhn, *The Structure of Scientific Revolutions*, University of Chicago Press, 1962. For a number of papers debating the conflict between Popper and Kuhn, see I. Lakatos and A. Musgrave, *Criticism and the Growth of Knowledge*, Cambridge University Press, 1970.
3. W.O. Hagstrom, *The Scientific Community*, Basic Books, 1965, pp. 69–104.
4. P. Medawar, "Is the scientific paper a fraud?" in D. Edge, ed., *Experiment*, B.B.C., 1964, pp. 7–12.
5. J.E. Myers, "Unleashing the untrained: some observations of student ethnographers", *Human Organization*, Summer 1969, pp. 155–60.
6. C.H. McCaghy and J.K. Skipper, "Lesbian behaviour as an adaptation to the occupation of stripping", *Social Problems*, Fall 1969, pp. 262–70; and J.K. Skipper and C.H. McCaghy, "Stripteasers: the anatomy and career contingencies of a deviant occupation", *Social Problems*, Winter 1970, pp. 391–405.
7. But see P.E. Hammond, *Sociologists at Work*, Basic Books, 1964.
8. J.S. Coleman, in Hammond, *op.cit.*, pp. 184–211.
9. H. Blumer, *An Appraisal of Thomas and Znaniecki's 'The Polish Peasant in Europe and America'*, Social Science Research Council, p. 83 and pp. 103–6.
10. *Children and Their Primary Schools* (Plowden Report), H.M.S.O., 1966, pp. 189–202.
11. W.I. Beveridge, *The Art of Scientific Investigation*, Heinemann, 1950, pp. 27–44.

12. B. Barber and R. Short, "The case of the floppy-eared rabbits: an instance of serendipity gained and serendipity lost", *American Journal of Sociology*, 1958, pp. 128–36.

CHAPTER 2. SOCIAL SCIENCE

1. The view of social science that follows is drawn from the work of Alfred Schutz. See, for example, "The problem of rationality in the social world" and "Concept and theory formation in the social sciences", pp. 89–114 and 1–19 respectively in D. Emmet and A. MacIntyre, *Sociological Theory and Philosophical Analysis*, Macmillan, 1970. A full account can be found in A. Schutz, *The Phenomenology of the Social World*, Evanston, 1967.
2. *Ibid.*
3. H.P. Rickman, *Understanding and the Social Sciences*, Heinemann, 1967, pp. 24–36.
4. N.K. Denzin, "Symbolic interactionism and ethnomethodology: a proposed synthesis", *American Sociological Review*, 1970, pp. 922–34.
5. For example, E. Goffman, *The Presentation of Self in Everyday Life*, Doubleday, 1959.
6. H. Garfinkel, "The rational properties of scientific and common sense activities", *Behavioural Science*, Jan. 1960, pp. 72–83.
7. A. Schutz, *Collected Papers*, vol. 1: *On the Methodology of the Social Sciences*, The Hague, 1967, pp. 3–96.
8. S. Schoeffler, *The Failures of Economics : a diagnostic study*, Harvard University Press, 1955, pp. 40–1.
9. A.V. Cicourel, *Method and Measurement in Sociology*, Free Press, 1964 especially pp. 39–72. This argument of Cicourel, itself drawing on Schutz, *op.cit.*, is only one view of the status of Sociology and the social sciences. Emmet and MacIntyre, *op. cit.*, contains other views.
10. B.G. Glaser and A.L. Strauss, *The Discovery of Grounded Theory*, Weidenfeld & Nicolson, 1968.
11. J. Holt, *How Children Fail*, Pitman, 1964.
12. D.F. Swift, "Educational psychology, sociology and environment: a controversy at cross-purposes", *British Journal of Sociology*, 1965, pp. 334–50 is an excellent introduction for those interested in Education.

13. D.F. Swift and H. Acland, "The Sociology of Education in Britain, 1960–1968: a bibliographical review", paper presented at the European Seminar on the Sociology of Education held at Noordwijk aan Zee, Netherlands, 1968.
14. *Ibid.* see also M.W. Riley, *Sociological Research*, Harcourt, Brace & World, 1963, pp. 703–9.
15. J. Bowlby, *Child Care and the Growth of Love*, Penguin, 1965.
16. B. Wootton, *Social Science and Social Pathology*, Allen & Unwin, 1959.
17. M.D. Ainsworth *et al.*, *Deprivation of Maternal Care : a reassessment of its effects*, Geneva, W.H.O., 1962.
18. M. Gluckman, *Closed Systems and Open Minds*, Oliver & Boyd, 1964.

CONTROVERSY 1. *Should scientists investigate sensitive social problems?*

1. A.R. Jensen, "How much can we boost IQ and scholastic achievement?" *Harvard Ed. Rev.*, Winter 1969, pp. 1–123. For a similar British view see C. Burt, "Intelligence and heredity", *New Scientist*, 1 May 1969, pp. 226–8.
2. *Harvard Ed. Rev.*, Spring 1969.
3. *Harvard Ed. Rev.*, Summer 1969, pp. 449–83.
4. W.F. Brazziel, "A letter from the South", *Harvard Ed. Rev.*, Spring 1969, p. 348.
5. *Ibid.*
6. M.K. Barry, letter to *New Society*, 24 June 1971, p. 1108.
7. Brazziel, *op. cit.*
8. A.R. Jensen, "Do schools cheat minority children?", *Educational Research,* vol. 14, no. 1, Nov. 1971, pp. 3–28. This article was advertised to appear in *Educational Research* for November 1971, after this typescript was completed and after the criticisms of the NFER appeared.
9. M. Morris, quoted in B. Hill, "NFER attacked over Jensen article", *The Times Educational Supplement*, 17 Sept. 1971, p. 5.
10. D. Pidgeon, quoted in Hill *ibid*; see also letters to *The Times Ed. Supp.* 1 Oct. 1971, p. 20.
11. H.J. Eysenck, *Race, Intelligence and Education*, M. Temple Smith, 1971.
12. See particularly *New Society* 24 June 1971 and 1 July 1971, pp. 29–30.

13. L. Hudson, Review of Eysenck's *Race, Intelligence and Education*, *New Society*, 1 July 1971, pp. 29–30.
14. W.F. Bodmer and L.L. Cavalli-Sforza, "Intelligence and race", *Scientific American*, Oct. 1970, pp. 19–29.
15. As a moderate illustration see H. Gans, "Where sociologists have failed", in N.K. Denzin, *The Values of Social Science*, Trans-action Books, 1970, pp. 83–6.

CHAPTER 3. QUESTIONS OF AUTHOR, SUBJECT AND DATE

1. See G. Hoinville and R. Jowell, "What happened in the election?" *New Society*, 2 July 1970, pp. 12–14.
2. This was A.H. Bowley, *The Natural Development of the Child*, E. and S. Livingstone, 1942, reprinted 1963. This book includes the work of Gesell, Isaacs and Buhler, and early work of Piaget.
3. J. Floud, A.H. Halsey and F.M. Martin, *Social Class and Educational Opportunity*, Heinemann, 1956.
4. J. Hemming, *Problems of Adolescent Girls*, Heinemann, 1960.
5. T. Tapper, *Young People and Society*, Faber, 1971.
6. D.H. Hargreaves, *Social Relations in a Secondary School*, Routledge & Kegan Paul, 1967.
7. J.W.B. Douglas and J.M. Blomfield, *Children Under Five*, Allen & Unwin, 1958.
8. J.W.B. Douglas, *The Home and the School*, MacGibbon & Kee, 1964.
9. J.W.B. Douglas, *All Our Future*, Davies, 1968.
10. W. Brandis and D. Henderson, *Social Class Language and Communication*, Routledge & Kegan Paul, 1970.
11. E.H. Carr, *What is History?*, Penguin, 1964, pp. 20–30.
12. E.G. West, *Education and the State*, Inst. of Econ. Affairs, 1965.
13. A.C.F. Beales *et al. Education: a framework for choice*, Inst. of Econ. Affairs, 1967.
14. M. Mead, *Coming of Age in Samoa*, Cape 1929, Penguin, 1943; M. Mead, *Growing Up in New Guinea*, Routledge & Kegan Paul, 1931, Penguin 1942.
15. Li An-Che, "Zuni. Some observations and queries", *American Anthropology* vol. 39, 1937, pp. 62–76.
16. E.H. Sutherland, *White Collar Crime*, Holt, Rinehart & Winston, 1949. First article was "White collar criminality", *Am. Soc. Rev.* Feb. 1940, pp. 1–12.

17. See, for example, E.M. Lemert, *Human Deviance, Social Problems and Social Control*, Prentice-Hall, 1967.
18. I.L. Horowitz, *The Rise and Fall of Project Camelot*, Massachusetts Institute of Technology Press, 1967; see also G. Sjoberg, *Ethics, Politics and Social Research*, Routledge & Kegan Paul, 1969, pp. 141–61.
19. Hagstrom, *op.cit.* (ch. 1, n. 3.), pp. 9–68.
20. R.K. Merton, "Priorities in scientific discovery" in B. Barber and W. Hirsch, *The Sociology of Science*, Free Press, 1962, pp. 447–85.
21. I.L. Horowitz, "The natural history of 'Revolution in Brazil'; a biography of a book", in Sjoberg, *op. cit.*, pp. 198–224.
22. J. Ford, *Social Class and the Comprehensive School*, Routledge & Kegan Paul, 1969, pp. vii and viii.
23. Horowitz, *The Rise and Fall of Project Camelot*, *op. cit.*
24. Z.A. Medvedev, *The Rise and Fall of T.D. Lysenko*, Columbia University Press, 1969.
25. See *The Times Ed. Supp.* 7 Aug. 1970, p. 1, and *The Times Ed. Supp.*, 21 Aug. 1970, p. 10.
26. J.D. Watson, *The Double Helix*, Weidenfeld & Nicolson, 1968.
27. J.S. Weiner, *The Piltdown Forgery*, Oxford University Press, 1955.
28. *Higher Education* (Robbins Report), H.M.S.O., 1963.
29. *Half our Future* (Newsom Report), H.M.S.O., 1963.
30. D.S. Greenberg, *The Politics of American Science*, Penguin, 1969, pp. 219–60.

CONTROVERSY 2. *Can young people make transitive inferences?*

1. See G. Matthews, "Piaget and his critics: part two", *The Times Ed. Supp.*, 10 Sept. 1971, p. 4.
2. P.E. Bryant and T. Trabasso, "Transitive inferences and memory in young children", *Nature*, vol. 232, 13 August 1971, pp. 456–8.
3. National Foundation for Educational Research, *Educational Research News*, no. 7, Sept. 1969, pp. 2–3.
4. J. Holt, "Ask a silly question", *The Times Ed. Supp.*, 17 July 1970, p. 4.
5. D. Elkind and J.H. Flavell, eds., *Studies in Cognitive Development*, Oxford University Press, 1969, p. xviii.
6. See *Observer* 22 Aug. 1971, p. 4, and 12 Sept. 1971, p. 7.
7. See *Daily Telegraph*, 23 Aug. 1971. For an account of the press reports following the original article in the *Observer* on 22 Aug. 1971, see *The Times Ed. Supp.*, 10 Sept. 1971, p. 80.

8. *Observer*, 12 Sept. 1971, p. 7.
9. See, for example, *Children and their Primary Schools, op. cit.* (ch. 1, n. 10), p. 142.

CHAPTER 4. SAMPLING

1. Schools Council, *Enquiry Number 1, Young School Leavers,* H.M.S.O., 1968.
2. J.H. Goldthorpe *et al., The Affluent Worker : industrial attitudes and behaviour,* Cambridge University Press, 1968.
3. Floud *et al., op. cit.* (ch. 3, n. 3).
4. B. Jackson and B. Marsden, *Education and the Working Class,* Routledge & Kegan Paul, 1962.
5. Hargreaves, *op. cit.* (ch. 3, n. 6).
6. J. Wakeford, *The Cloistered Elite,* Macmillan, 1969.
7. M. Young and P. Willmott, *Family and Kinship in East London,* Routledge & Kegan Paul, 1957, Penguin 1962; and *Family and Class in a London Suburb,* Routledge & Kegan Paul, 1960, Penguin, 1964.
8. M.D. Shipman, "Environmental influences on response to questionnaies", *British Journal of Educational Psychology,* 1967.
9. Wakeford, *op. cit.*
10. S. Isaacs, *Social Development in Young Children,* Routledge & Kegan Paul, 9th impression, 1964.
11. A.C. Kinsey *et al., Sexual Behaviour in the Human Female,* W.B. Saunders, 1953, pp. 58–100.
12. T. Veness, *School Leavers,* Methuen, 1962, pp. 1–25.
13. M. Phillips, *Small Social Groups in England,* Methuen, 1965, pp. 3–19.
14. Hemming, *op.cit.* (ch. 3, n. 4).
15. For this and other blunders, see L. Rogers, *The Pollsters,* Knopf, 1949.
16. R.R. Dale, *Mixed or Single-sex School?,* Routledge & Kegan Paul, 1969.
17. J. Gabriel, *The Emotional Problems of the Teacher in the Classroom,* F.W. Cheshire (Melbourne), 1957.
18. F. Musgrove, *Youth and the Social Order,* Routledge & Kegan Paul, 1964.
19. J. Newson and E. Newson, *Infant Care in an Urban Community,* Allen & Unwin, 1968.

20. P. Willmott, *Adolescent Boys of East London*, Routledge & Kegan Paul, 1966.
21. D. Glass, ed., *Social Mobility in Britain*, Routledge & Kegan Paul, 1954.
22. M.L. Kellmer Pringle *et al.*, *11,000 Seven-Year-Olds*, Longmans, 1966.
23. Douglas *op.cit.*, three books (ch. 3, nn. 7, 8, 9).
24. F.W. Miller *et al.*, *Growing up in Newcastle upon Tyne*, Oxford University Press, 1960.
25. T.W. Adorno *et al.*, *The Authoritarian Personality*, Harper Bros. 1960. See also Chapter 7. See also H.H. Hyman and P.B. Sheatsley, "The authoritarian personality – a methodological critique", in R. Christie and M. Jahoda, *Studies in the Scope and Method of "The Authoritarian Personality"*, Free Press, 1954, pp. 50–122.

CHAPTER 5. STUDIES BASED ON OBSERVATION

1. R. Rosenthal and K.L. Fode, "The effect of experimenter bias on the performance of albino rats", *Behavioural Science*, 1963, pp. 183–9.
2. I. Firth, "*N*-rays – ghost of a scandal past", *New Scientist*, 25 Dec. 1969, pp. 642–3. H.J. Eysenck, *Fact and Fiction in Psychology*, Penguin, 1965, pp. 127–130. I.J. Good, *The Scientist Speculates*, Heinemann, 1962, Index.
3. A.J. Reiss, "Stuff and Nonsense about social surveys and observations", in H.S. Becker *et al*, *Institution and the Person*, Aldine Press, 1968, pp. 351–367.
4. R. Frankenberg, "Participant observation", *New Society*, 7 March 63, pp. 22–3.
5. H. Gans, "The participant observer as a human being", in Becker *et al.*, *op.cit.*, pp. 300–17.
6. A. Vidich, J. Bensman and M.R. Stein, eds., *Reflections on Community Studies*, Wiley, 1964.
7. J.R. Seeley, "Crestwood Heights: intellectual and libidinal dimensions of research", in Vidich *et al.*, *op.cit.*, pp. 157–206.
8. M.R. Stein, "The eclipse of community: some glances at the education of a sociologist", in Vidich *et al.*, *op. cit.*, pp. 207–32.
9. K.H. Wolff, "Surrender and community study: the study of Loma", in Vidich *et al.*, *op.cit.*, pp. 233–64.

10. W.F. Whyte, *Street Corner Society*, University of Chicago Press, enlarged edition, 1954, pp. 279–360.
11. A.J. Vidich, "Freedom and responsibility in research: a rejoinder", *Human Organization*, Spring 1960, pp. 3–4.
12. I. Festinger *et al.*, *When Prophecy Fails*, University of Minnesota Press, 1956.
13. R.F. Bales, *Interaction Process Analysis*, Addison-Wesley, 1950.
14. Hargreaves, *op. cit.* (ch. 3, n. 6), pp. 193–205.

CONTROVERSY 3. *Do the public want religions education in state schools?*

1. R. Goldman, "Do we want our children taught about God?", *New Society*, 27 May 1965, pp. 8–10.
2. British Humanist Society, *N.O.P. Survey*, 1969.
3. Schools Council, *op.cit.* (ch. 4, n. 1).
4. *The Fourth R* (The Durham Report), S.P.C.K., 1970, pp. 96–7.

CHAPTER 6. INFORMATION THROUGH ASKING QUESTIONS

1. R. Jowell and G. Hoinville, "Opinion polls tested", *New Society*, 7 Aug. 1969, pp. 206–7.
2. R. Blackburn, "A brief guide to bourgeois ideology", in A. Cockburn and R. Blackburn, *Student Power*, Penguin 1969, pp. 199–200.
3. N. Gross, W.S. Mason and A.W. McEachern, *Explorations in Role Analysis*, Wiley, 1966.
4. S.L. Payne, *The Art of Asking Questions*, Princeton University Press, 1951.
5. A. Smithers and S. Carlisle, "Reluctant teachers", *New Society*, 5 March 1970, pp. 391–2.
6. Shipman, *op. cit.* (ch. 4, n. 8).
7. Adorno, *op.cit.* (ch. 4, n. 25) and Hyman and Sheatsley, *op.cit.* (ch. 4, n. 25).
8. E. Frenkel-Brunswick, in Hyman and Sheatsley, *ibid*, pp. 226–75.
9. E.Z. Vogt and R. Hyman, *Water Witching U.S.A.*, University of Chicago Press, 1959, pp. 92–9.
10. Kinsey, *op.cit.* (ch. 4, n. 11).
11. Government Social Survey, *Handbook for Interviewers*, H.M.S.O.
12. C.A. Moser, *Survey Methods in Social Investigation*, Heinemann, 1958, pp. 193–4.

13. J. Durbin and A. Stuart, "Differences in response rates of experienced and inexperienced interviewers", *J. Roy. Statistical Society*, 1951, pp. 163–205.
14. F. Zweig, *The Quest for Fellowship*, Heinemann, 1965, pp. 1–33.
15. J. Rich, *Interviewing Children and Adolescents*, Macmillan, 1968.
16. J. Holt, "Ask a silly question", *The Times Ed. Supp.*, 17 July 1970, p. 4.
17. P. Townsend, *The Last Refuge*, Routledge & Kegan Paul, 1962, pp. 3–16; see also P. Townsend, *The Family Life of Old People*, Routledge & Kegan Paul, 1957, pp. 3–10.

CONTROVERSY 4. *Is the initial teaching alphabet better than the traditional?*

1. In this controversy i.t.a. refers to the initial teaching alphabet. t.o. refers to traditional orthography.
2. J.A. Downing, *The i.t.a. Reading Experiment*, Evans Bros, 1964. The second was J.A. Downing and B. Jones, "Some problems of evaluating i.t.a.: a second experiment", *Educational Research*, Feb. 1966. pp. 100–14.
3. V. Southgate, "Approaching i.t.a.", *Ed. Res.*, Feb. 1965, pp. 83–96.
4. Downing and Jones, *op.cit.*
5. F.W. Warburton and V. Southgate, *i.t.a.: An Indepedent Evaluation*, J. Murray and W. & R. Chambers, 1969.
6. *The Times Ed. Supp.*, 26 Dec. 1969, p. 28.
7. See, for example, J. Downing, *The i.t.a. symposium*, N.F.E.R. 1967.

CHAPTER 7. EXPERIMENTS

1. T. Hirschi and H.C. Selvin, *Delinquency Research*, Free Press, 1967, pp. 8–33; see also B. Wootton, *Social Science and Social Pathology*, Allen & Unwin, 1969, pp. 81–135.
2. F.J. Roethlisberger and W.J. Dickson, *Management and the Worker*, Wiley, 1939.
3. A. Carey, "The Hawthorne Studies: a radical analysis", *Am. Soc. Rev.*, 1967, pp. 403–16.
4. M. Young and P. McGeeney, *Learning Begins at Home*, Routledge & Kegan Paul, 1968, pp. 87–106.
5. H.G. Canady, "The effect of 'Rapport' on the I.Q.: a new approach to the problem of racial psychology", *J. Negro Studies*, 1936, pp. 208–19.

6. A. Rabin, W. Nelson and M. Clark, "Rorschach content as a function of perceptual experience and sex of examiner", *Journal of Clinical Psychology*, 1954, pp. 188–90.
7. J. Masling, "The influence of situational and interpersonal variables in projective testing", *Psychol. Bulletin*, 1960. pp. 65–85.
8. J. Masling, "Effect of warm and cold interaction on the administration and scoring of an intelligence test", *Journal of Consulting Psychology*, 1959, pp. 336–41.
9. M.T. Orne, "On the social psychology of the psychological experiment", *Am. Psych.*, 1962, pp. 776–83.
10. N. Friedman, *The Social Nature of Psychological Research*, Basic Books, 1967, contains many examples of this type of confusion.
11. E. Goffman, *Encounters*, Bobbs Merrill, 1961.
12. R. Rosenthal, *Experimenter Effects in Behavioural Research*, Appleton-Century-Crofts, 1966.
13. R. Rosenthal and L. Jacobson, *Pygmalion in the Classroom*, Holt, Rinehart & Winston, 1968.
14. W.L. Claiborn, "Expectancy effects in the classroom: a failure to replicate", *Journal of Educational Psychology*, vol. 60, 1969, pp. 377–83.
15. Friedman, *op.cit.*, pp. 33–69.
16. M.T. Orne, "The nature of hypnosis: artifact and essence", *Journal of Abnormal Social Psychology*, 1959, pp. 277–99.
17. L.M. Terman, *Genetic Studies of Genius*, vol. 1., Stanford University Press, 1926.
18. H.H. Hughes and H.D. Converse, "Characteristics of the gifted: a case for a sequel to Terman's study", *Exceptional Child*, 1962, pp. 179–83.
19. J.W.B. Douglas, *op.cit.* (ch. 3. nn. 7–9, especially n. 8).
20. C. Burt, critical notice in *B.J.E.P.*, June 1965, pp. 259–264.
21. G. Horobin, D. Oldman and B. Bytheway, "The social differentiation of ability", *Sociology*, May 1967, pp. 113–29.

CONTROVERSY 5. *The Reformation and the schools*

1. A.F. Leach, *The Schools of Medieval England*, Methuen, 1916.
2. J. Simon, "A.F. Leach on the Reformation, 1", *B.J.E.S.*, May 1955, pp. 128–143 and "11", *British Journal of Educational Studies*. Nov. 1955, pp. 32–48; and *Education and Society in Tudor England*, Cambridge University Press, 1966.

3. W.N. Chaplin, "A.F. Leach: a re-appraisal", *B.J.E.S.*, May 1963, pp. 99–124.
4. W.K. Jordan, *Philanthropy in England 1480–1660*, Allen & Unwin, 1959.
5. F.J. Fisher, Book review, *Brit. J. Soc.*, March 1960, pp. 188–9.

CHAPTER 8. DOCUMENTS AND OTHER UNOBTRUSIVE MEASURES

1. L. Gottschalk, C. Kluckhohn and R. Angell, 'The use of personal documents in history', *Anthropology and Sociology*, S.S.R.C. 1951, pp. 3–75.
2. Home Office, *Report of the Departmental Committee on Criminal Statistics* (Chairman: M.W. Perks), Cmnd. 3448, 1967.
3. H. Mannheim, *Comparative Criminology*, Vol. 1., Routledge & Kegan Paul, 1965, p. 114.
4. Home Office, *op.cit.* pp. 10–11.
5. Mannheim, *op.cit.*, pp. 98–118, for a discussion of the reliability of statistics.
6. A.V. Cicourel, *The Social Organization of Juvenile Justice*, Wiley, 1967.
7. *Ibid.* pp. 26–9. See also J. Kitsuse and A.V. Cicourel, "A note on the uses of official statistics", *Social Problems*, 1963, pp. 131–9.
8. Cicourel, *op.cit.*
9. W.I. Thomas and F. Znaniecki, *The Polish Peasant in Europe and America*, 2 volume edition, 1927.
10. Blumer, *op. cit.* (ch. 1, n. 9), pp. 28–53.
11. *Ibid*, pp. 74–6 and 109–10.
12. *Ibid.*
13. E.J. Webb *et al*, *Unobtrusive Measures*, Rand McNally, 1966.
14. C. Madge and H. Jennings, *May the Twelfth, Mass Observation Day Surveys*, Faber, 1937.

CONTROVERSY 6. *To stream or unstream?*

1. J.C. Barker Lunn, *Streaming in the Primary School*, N.F.E.R., 1970.
2. I.E. Finch, "A study of the personal and social consequence of groups of secondary schooling of the experience of different methods of allocation within secondary courses", M.A. thesis, University of London, 1954.

3. W.G.A. Rudd, "The psychological effects of streaming by attainment with special reference to a group of selected children", *B.J.E.P.*, 1956, pp. 47–60.
4. J.S. Blandford, "Standardised tests in junior schools with special reference to the effects of streaming on the consistency of results", *B.J.E.P.*, 1958, pp. 170–3.
5. J.M. Morris, *Standards and Progress in Reading*, N.F.E.R., 1966.
6. J.C. Daniels, "Some effects of segregation and streaming on the intellectual and scholastic development of Junior School children", Ph.D. thesis, University of Nottingham, 1959.
7. A. Yates and D.A. Pidgeon, "The effects of streaming", *Ed. Res.*, Nov. 1959.
8. B. Simon, "*Non-streaming in the Junior School*", Forum, 1964.
9. Douglas, *op.cit.* (ch. 3, n. 8).
10. B. Jackson, *Streaming*, Routledge & Kegan Paul, 1964.
11. Barker Lunn, *op.cit.*
12. M. Goldberg, *et al.*, *Effects of Ability Grouping*, Columbia University Press, 1966.
13. R.B. Ekstrom, *Experimental Studies of Homogenous Grouping: a review of the literature*, Princeton University Press, 1959.
14. See S. Maclure, *Education*, 2 May 1969.
15. A. Yates, *Grouping in Education*, Hamburg, Unesco Institute for Education, 1966, pp. 131–2. See also T. Husen, *International Study of Achievement in Mathematics*, Stockholm, Almquist & Wicksell, 1967.
16. Surrey Educational Research Association, *To Stream or not to Stream*, 1968.
17. E. Ferri, *Streaming: two years later*, N.F.E.R., 1971.
18. C. Benn, "Against the stream", *New Society*, 5 Aug. 1971, pp. 252–3.

CHAPTER 9. THE PRESENTATION OF EVIDENCE

1. Newsom Report, *op.cit.* and Robbins Report, *op.cit.* (ch. 3, nn. 29, 28).
2. See, for example, J.R. Amos *et al. Statistical Concepts*, Harper & Row, 1965.
3. For example, W.J. Reichmann, *Use and Abuses of Statistics*, Methuen, 1961.

4. For example, H. Miner, "Researchmanship: the feedback of expertise", *Human Organization*, Spring 1960, pp. 1–3.
5. S. Labovitz, "The nonutility of significance tests: the significance of tests of significance reconsidered", *Pacific Sociological Review*, 1970, pp. 141–8.
6. D. Gold, "Statistical tests and substantive significance", *American Sociologist*, 1969, pp. 42–6.
7. H.C. Selvin, "A critique of tests of significance in survey research", *Am. Soc. Rev.*, 1957, pp. 519–27.
8. J.S. Coleman, letter, *American Journal of Sociology*, 1958, pp. 59–60.
9. S.F. Camilleri, "Theory, probability and induction in social research", *Am. Soc. Rev.*, 1962, pp. 170–8.
10. E. Gowers, *The Complete Plain Words*, Penguin edn., 1962, p. 69.
11. Extracted from A. Kohn, "Principles and methods of obscuratism", *New Scientist*, 29 Jan. 1970.
12. B. Cane and C. Schroeder, *The Teacher and Research*, N.F.E.R. 1970, p. 39.
13. V. Southgate and G.R. Roberts, *Reading – Which Approach?*, University of London Press, 1970.
14. D. Lawton, *Social Class, Language and Education*, Routledge & Kegan Paul, 1968, pp. 77–102; see "Comment" sections.
15. The first published account was, "Some sociological determinants of perception. An inquiry into sub-cultural differences", *Brit. J. Soc.* 1958.
16. Examples of such ploys can be found in I.V. Good, *The Scientist Speculates*, Heinemann, 1962. Kohn, *op.cit.* is also useful.
17. J.W.N. Watkins, "Confession is good for ideas", in D. Edge, ed., *Experiment*, B.B.C., 1964, pp. 64–70.
18. M.T. Oldcom, "The ABC's of groupness", *J. Abnormal Sociology*, vol. 5, pp. 6–45, reported in Miner, *op. cit.*
19. Cane and Schroeder, *op. cit.*, pp. 36–45.

CONTROVERSY 7. *How prejudiced are the British?*

1. R. Moore, "Race relations and the rediscovery of sociology", *Brit. J. Soc.*, March 1971, pp. 97–104.
2. Institute of Race Relations, E.J.B. Rose, ed., *Colour and Citizenship*, Oxford University Press 1969.

3. J. Rex., "The ethics of research", *New Society*, 7 Aug. 1969, p. 221.
4. Correspondence columns of *New Society*, 14 and 21 Aug., 4 and 11 Sept. 1969.
5. *New Society*, 14 Aug. 1969, p. 262, letter of Rowan J. *New Society* 21 Aug. 1969, pp. 300–1, letter of D. Lawrence.
6. *New Society*, 4 Sept. 1969, pp. 371–2, letter of M. Abrams.
7. *New Society*, 11 Sept. 1969, p. 408, letters of D. Lawrence and J. Rowan.
8. J. Rex and R. Moore, *Race, Community and Conflict*, Oxford University Press, 1967.
9. J.G. Davies and J. Taylor, "Race, community and no conflict", *New Society*, 9 July 1970, pp. 67–9.
10. See Davies and Taylor, *op. cit.* Correspondence is in *New Society*, 16, 23 and 30 July 1970.

CHAPTER 10. THE INTERPRETATION OF RESULTS

1. M.C. Wittrock, "The learning-by-discovery hypothesis", in L.S. Shulman and E.R. Kinslar, *Learning by Discovery*, Rand McNally, 1966, pp. 33–75.
2. "Wisconsin studies of the measurement and prediction of teacher effectiveness," *Journal of Experimental Education*, Sept. 1961, pp. 5–156.
3. K. Lewin, R. Lippitt and R.K. White, "Patterns of aggressive behaviour in experimentally created social climates", in E. Amidon and J. Hough, *Interaction Analysis*, Addison-Wesley, 1967, pp. 24–46.
4. R. Lippitt and R.K. White, "An experimental study of leadership and group life" in H.P. Proshansky and B. Seidenberg, *Basic Studies in Social Psychology*, Holt, Rinehart & Winston, 1965, pp. 523–37.
5. Lewin *et al.*, *op.cit.* p. 37.
6. S. Wiseman, *Education and Environment*, University of Manchester Press, 1964, pp. 55–73 and 178–9.
7. *Ibid.*; see also Swift and Acland, *op.cit.* (ch. 2, n. 13) p. 3.
8. H.R. Alker, "A typology of ecological fallacies", in M. Dogan and S. Rokkan, *Quantitative Ecological Analysis in the Social Sciences*, Massachusetts Institute of Technology Press, 1969.

9. M.W. Riley, *Sociological Research*, Vol. 1, Harcourt, Brace & World, 1963, pp. 700–9.
10. For examples see discussion by D.S. Pugh, "Organizations: their nature", in F.D. Carver and J.J. Sergiovanni, *Organizations and Human Behaviour*, McGraw-Hill, 1969, pp. 111–29.
11. F. Musgrove and P.H. Taylor, *Society and the Teacher's Role*, Routledge & Kegan Paul, 1969.
12. P.E. Daunt, review of Musgrove and Taylor (above, n. 11) in *Universities Quarterly*, Autumn 1969, pp. 479–81.
13. Jordan, *op.cit.* (Contro 5, n. 4).
14. D. Riesman, *The Lonely Crowd*, Doubleday, 1953.
15. E. Larrabee, "David Riesman and his readers", in S.M. Lipset and L. Lowenthal, *Character and Social Structure*, Free Press, 1961.
16. D. Riesman and N. Glazer, "A reconsideration", in Lipset and Lowenthal, pp. 419–58.
17. J.W. Wiggins and H. Schoeck, "A profile of the aged: U.S.A.", *Geriatrics*, July 1961, pp. 336–42.
18. L.D. Cain, "The AMA and the gerontologists: uses and abuses of 'A profile of the aged: U.S.A.'", in Sjoberg *op.cit.* (ch. 3, n. 18), pp. 78–114.
19. J.W. Wiggins and H. Schoeck, *Scientism and Values*, Van Nostrand, 1960.

CONTROVERSY 8. *The priority given to reducing the size of school classes*

1. C. Fleming, "Class size as a variable in the teaching situation", *Ed. Res.*, Feb. 1959, pp. 35–48.
2. P. Rossi, "Evaluating social action programmes", in N. Denzin, *The Values of Social Science*, Trans-action Books, 1970, pp. 89–90.
3. T. Husen, *International Study of Achievement in Mathematics*, Almquist and Wicksell, Stockholm, 1967, pp. 277–83.
4. A. Little and J. Russell, paper read at the U.K. Reading Association Conference, 1971: see *The Times Ed. Supp.*, 30 Sept. 1971, p. 5.
5. Morris *op.cit.* (Contro 6, n. 5), pp. 93–5 and 223–4.
6. R. Davie, "The child, the school and the home". Paper read at the Annual meeting of the British Association for the Advancement of Science (Education section), 3 Sept. 1970; paper kindly provided by the author.

7. *Children and their Primary Schools* (Plowden Report), *op.cit.* (ch. 1, n. 10), pp. 279–82.

CHAPTER 11. GENERALIZATION AND POLICY

1. M. Schofield, *The Sexual Behaviour of Young People*, Longmans, 1965.
2. Jackson and Marsden, *op.cit.* (ch. 4, n. 4).
3. Blumer, *op.cit.* (ch. 1, n. 9).
4. Institute of Race Relations, *op.cit.* (Contro. 7, n. 2), pp. 588–603.
5. A.B. Cherns, "Social sciences and policy", *Soc. Rev.*, Monograph 16 Sept. 1970, p. 56.
6. F.R. Harris, ed., *Social Science and National Policy*, Trans-action Books, 1970, p. 3.
7. Institute of Race Relations, *op.cit.* (Contro. 7, n. 2).
8. E. Charles, "The effect of present trends in fertility and mortality upon the future population of Great Britain and upon its age composition", in L. Hogben, *Political Arithmetic*, Allen & Unwin, 1938, pp. 73–105.
9. E.M. Hubback, *The Population of Britain*, Penguin, 1947, pp. 39–42.
10. *Royal Commission on Population, Report*, Cmnd 7695, 1949, pp. 80–92.
11. Central Office of Information, *Monthly Digest of Statistics*, April 1966, p. 12.
12. Central Statistical Office, *Monthly Digest of Statistics*, April 1969, pp. 16–17.
13. R. Layard *et al.*, *The Impact of Robbins*, Penguin, 1969.
14. *Committee to consider the future numbers of medical practitioners and the appropriate intake of medical students* (Willink Committee), H.M.S.O., 1957.
15. R.H.S. Crossman, *Paying for the Social Services*, Fabian Society, 1969.
16. J.S. Coleman, *Equality of Educational Opportunity*, U.S. Dept. of Health, Education and Welfare, 1966.
17. G.C. Cain and H.W. Watts, "Problems in making policy inferences from the Coleman Report", *Am. Soc. Rev.*, April 1970, pp. 228–42.
18. J.S. Coleman, "Reply to Cain and Watts", *Am. Soc. Rev.*, April 1970, pp. 242–9.
19. D.J. Aigner, "A comment on problems of making inferences from the Coleman Report", *Am. Soc. Rev.*, April 1970, pp. 249–52.

20. Plowden Report, *op.cit.* (ch. 1, n. 10). See also Glennerster, H., "The Plowden Research", *Journal of the Royal Statistical Society*, Series A, 1969, pp. 194–204.
21. Rosenthal and Jacobson, *op.cit.* (ch. 7, n. 13).
22. T. Barber and M. Silver, "Fact, fiction and the experimenter bias effect", *Psych. Bull.*, vol. 70, 1968.
23. Claiborn, *op.cit.* (ch. 7, n. 14).

CHAPTER 12. THE SCOPE OF SOCIAL SCIENCE

1. See, for example, Blackburn *op.cit.* (ch. 6, n. 2).
2. A.V. Gouldner, "Anti-Minotaur: the myth of value-free sociology", *Social Problems*, vol. 9, 1962, pp. 199–213.
3. C.W. Mills, *The Sociological Imagination*, Oxford University Press, 1959, pp. 50–75.
4. W.G. Runciman, "Thinking by numbers", *The Times Literary Supp.*, 6 Aug. 1971, pp. 943–4.
5. Gouldner, *op.cit.*
6. Roethlisberger and Dickson, *op.cit.* (ch. 7, n. 2).
7. Carey, *op.cit.* (ch. 7, n. 3).
8. Lippitt and White, *op.cit.* (ch. 10, n. 4).
9. B.R. McCandless, *Children; Behaviour and Development*, Holt, Rinehart & Winston, 1967, p. 564.
10. J.A. Rex, "The spread of the pathology of natural science to the social sciences", *Soc. Rev.* Monograph No. 16, 1970, pp. 143–62.
11. W.D. Garvey and B.C. Griffith, "Scientific information exchange in psychology", *Science*, vol. 146, 1964, pp. 1955–9.
12. See D. Price, *Little Science, Big Science*, Columbia University Press, 1965. For examples of such informal communication see D. Crane, "The nature of scientific communication and influence", *International Social Science Journal*, vol. 22, no. 1, 1970, pp. 28–41.
13. R.D. Whitley, "The formal communication system of science", *Soc. Review* Monograph, No. 16, 1970, pp. 143–62.
14. A.B. Cherns, "Use of the social sciences", *Human Relations*, vol. 21, no. 4, 1968, pp. 313–25.
15. N. Chomsky, *American Power and the New Mandarins*, Chatto & Windus, 1969, pp. 7–129.
16. B.S. Greenberg, *The Politics of American Science*, Penguin, 1969, pp. 53–78.

17. Hagstrom, *op.cit.* (ch. 1, n. 3), pp. 254–91.
18. The list of roles has been drawn from N.K. and Denzin, *The Values of Social Science*, pp. 9–11, and P.F. Lazarsfeld *et al*, *The Uses of Sociology*, Weidenfeld & Nicolson, 1968, pp. xvii-xviii.
19. Schofield, *op.cit.*
20. Schools Council, *op.cit.* (ch. 4, n. 1).
21. A.W. Gouldner, *The Coming Crisis of Western Sociology*, Heinemann, 1971.
22. C.W. Mills, *The Power Elite*, Oxford University Press, 1959.
23. Chomsky, *op.cit.*, p. 22.
24. In the U.S.A. 3 to 5 per cent of natural scientists worked mainly in basic research, 8 per cent in applied research and 22 per cent in development.
25. Rex and Moore, *op.cit.* (Contro. 7, n. 8).
26. Brandis and Henderson, *op.cit.* (ch. 3, n. 10).
27. R. Fowler, "The rat-box philosophy", *Listener*, 30 Jan. 1969, pp. 140–2.

Index

Abrams, M., 131
Acland, H., 24, 139n
Adolescent Boys of East London, 59
Adorno, T.W., 60n
Aigner, D. J., 154n
Ainsworth, M.D., 26n
Alker, H.R., 140
American Miscellaneous Society, 46
Amos, J., 122n
Angell, R., 108n
Anthropology, 14, 27, 37, 65
Authoritarian Personality studies, 60, 82, 136

Bales, R.F., 69, 71
Barber, B., 10n, 39n
Barber, T., 156
Barker Lunn, J.C., 117n, 118n
Beales, A.C.F., 36n
Benn, C., 120n
Bensman, J., 68, 70
Bernstein, B., 124–5
Beveridge, W.I., 11n
Blackburn, R., 78, 159n
Blandford, J.S., 117
Blandot, Blondlot or Blondot, R or P or M., 64
Blumer, H., 8n, 113–14, 149n

Bodmer, W.F., 29–30
Booth, C., 122
Bowlby, J., 26
Boyle, R., 40
Brandis, W., 34n, 167
Brazziel, W.F., 28
British Humanist Association, 73–4
British Institute of Public Opinion, 85
British Journal of Educational Psychology, 128
British Journal of Psychology, 31
British Sociological Association, 130
Bryant, P.E., 48
Buhler, C., 33
Burt, C., 28n, 103
Bytheway, B., 103–4

Cain, G.C., 154n
Cain, L.D., 142n
Camelot, Project, 39–40
Camilleri, S.F., 123
Canady, H.G., 96
Cane, B., 124, 128
Carey, A., 95
Carlisle, S., 80n
Carr, E.H., 35

INDEX

Firth, I, 64n
Fisher, F.S., 106
Flavell, J.H., 48n
Fleming, A., 10
Fleming, C., 144
Floud, J., 33, 54
Fode, K.L., 63
Follow-up studies, 102–4
Ford, J., 40
Forum, 37, 117–18
Fowler, R., 167n
Frankenberg, R., 67
Frenkel-Brunswick, E., 82
Friedman, N., 97, 100
Fullbright, Senator, 166

Gabriel, J., 59
Gans, H., 30n, 67
Garfinkel, H., 15
Garvey, W.D., 161
Geriatrics, 142
Gesell, A., 33n
Glaser, B.G., 18
Glass, D., 59
Glazer, N., 142
Glennerster, H., 155n
Gluckman, M., 27n
Goffman, E., 15, 98
Gold, O., 122
Goldberg, M., 118n
Goldman, R., 73
Goldthorpe, J.H., 53
Good, I.V., 125n
Gottschalk, J., 108
Gouldner, A.V., 159, 163, 166
Government Social Survey, 52, 60–1, 74, 77, 84–5
Gowers, E., 123
Greenberg, D.S., 46n, 164n

Griffith, B.C., 161
Gross, N., 79
Growing up in Newcastle upon Tyne, 60

Hagstrom, W.O., 2n, 39, 164n
Halsey, A.H., 33, 54
Hammond, P.E., 7n
Hargreaves, D.H., 34, 55, 71
Harris, F.R., 150n
Harvard Educational Review, 28
Hawthorne effect, 94–108, 160
Hemming, J., 34, 58
Henderson, D., 34n, 167
Hill, B., 29n
Hirsch, W., 39n
Hirschi, T., 94n
History, 14–15, 17, 35, 101–2, 105–6, 108, 141
Hogben, L., 152n
Hoinville, G., 32n, 76
Holt, J., 18, 48n, 86–7
Home Office, 109–10
Hooke, R., 43
Horobin, G., 103–4
Horowitz, I.L., 39n, 40
Hubback, E.M., 152
Huberman, M., 42–3
Hudson, L., 29n
Hughes, H.H., 102–3
Husen, T., 118n, 144n
Huygens, C., 43
Hyman, H.H., 60n, 82
Hyman, R., 83

Ideal types, 135
Infant Care in an Urban Community, 59

Trow, M., 7

Unesco, 42–3
U.S.A., 39, 40, 42, 110, 118
U.S. Office of Education, 123, 154
U.S.S.R., 36, 41–2

Validity, x, xi, 32
Van Osten, 83
Vavilov, N.I., 41
Veness, T., 57
Victoria County Histories, 105
Vidich, A., 68, 70
Vinci, L. de, 65
Vogt, E.Z., 83n

Wakeford, J., 55
Wallace, Governor, 29
Warburton, F.W., 90–2
Watkins, J.W.N., 126
Watson, J.D., 43
Watt, J., 43
Watts, H.W., 154n
Webb, E.J., 115
Weiner, J.S., 44n

West, E.G., 36
When Prophecy Fails, 70
White, R.K., 136, 160
Whitley, R.D., 161–2
Whyte, W.F., 69–70, 71
Wiggins, J.W., 142–3
Willinck Committee, 153
Willmott, P., 55, 59
Wisconsin studies of teacher effec-
  tiveness, 134
Wiseman, S., 139
Wolff, K.H., 68
Woodward, A.S., 44
Wootton, B., 26

Yates, A., 117, 118n
Young, M., 55, 95n, 97
Young People and Society, 33
Young School Leavers, 52, 74, 166
Youth and the Social Order, 59

Zeigarnik, B.V., 40
Znaniecki, F., 8, 112–14, 136
Zweig, F., 85–6